the
cool
parents'
guide to new york

Excursions and Activities In and Around
Our City that Your Children Will Love and
You Won't Think Are Too Bad Either

Fourth Edition

Alfred Gingold and Helen Rogan

universe publishing

dedication

This book is for our son Toby, semper cool; and for up-and-comers Asa, Jasper, Milo, Magnolia, and Wolf.

First Universe edition published in the United States of America in 2003
by UNIVERSE PUBLISHING
a Division of Rizzoli International Publications, Inc.
300 Park Avenue South
New York, NY 10010
www.rizzoliusa.com

© 2008, 2003, 1998, and 1996 by Pearl Productions, Inc.
Interior and Cover Design by Paul Kepple at Headcase Design
Cover Illustration by Mary Lynn Blasutta

2010/ 10 9 8 7 6 5 4 3 2

Printed in the United States
Library of Congress Catalog Control Number: 2007909668

ISBN-13: 978-0-7893-1687-5

Publisher's Note: Neither Universe Publishing nor the author has any interest, financial or personal, in the locations listed in this book. While every effort was made to ensure that all data was accurate at the time of publication, we advise calling ahead or checking websites to confirm details.

table of contents

acknowledgments

For their help with this edition, we thank Sharlene Breakey, Melisa Coburn, Claire Gierczak, Chrissy Gillespie, Lee Anna Jackson, Caitlin Leffel, Charles Miers, Ellen Nidy, Meg Siesfeld, and Helene Silver.

—A.G. & H.R.

preface to the fourth edition

Much has changed since the first edition of this book appeared in 1996. The dancing chicken of Chinatown has gone to her reward and the Police Museum has moved twice. MoMA temporarily migrated to Queens, which became the new Brooklyn, which became the new Manhattan. MoMA has since moved back to its home in Manhattan, which still contains most of the city's most popular attractions, though one of them is a place you might hesitate to show your children: Ground Zero.

Yet in many ways, New York City remains the same as it ever was. It still crackles with a vitality that few cities on earth can match, and it still holds surprises, excitements, and pleasures that not even the most jaded, been-there-done-that New Yorkers can resist—and that goes for their kids as well.

introduction

What Is a Cool Parent?

A cool parent is one who does not view family activities intended for the child's enrichment as a vale of unrelenting boredom, typified by trips to diddly museums where an unemployed actress in a mobcap tells you about beeswax. The cool parent has higher aspirations involving enjoyment, pleasure, and fun.

This book addresses the reality of being a (cool) New York City parent: discriminating, inquisitive, pressed for time, wanting to know there will be decent food nearby, and, above all, that children and parents alike will have a good time. Everybody knows how much there is to do in our city. What New York parents need is a little help finding the best of both the familiar and the offbeat.

To that end, *The Cool Parents' Guide* offers a series of day trips, clusters of activities and sights, with enough variety and leeway within each to keep everybody happy. We tell you what to expect, what else there is to see or do in the vicinity and sometimes we recommend where to eat—but not when there are viable choices all around.

There are few childrens' museums in this book. They can be great for the kids, and you'll certainly visit your fair share of them before your parenting days are through, but no one in his or her right mind would claim childrens' museums are fun for adults.

Likewise, we do not dwell on attractions that seem to us already well known and utilized by New Yorkers, such as Central Park—which, if you haven't already visited, you really should. As devoted New Yorkers and parents ourselves, we guarantee all information for up-to-the-minute accuracy—but not a minute beyond.

At this point all you really need to decide is whether or not you are cool. Read our manifesto and see if you match the profile:

The Cool Parents' Manifesto

1. The cool parent demands the right, if only in principle, to enjoy family excursions, while acknowledging that this is not always possible (unless you're mad for cartoons or clowns). For some parents, coolness means never going to Disney-anything. So be it. (Although sometimes you do have to.)

2. The cool parent is mindful of the strategic importance of a cab, remembering the consequences of arriving at the appointed destination with kids already bored, exhausted, or whining.

3. To those whose idea of a keen time is bringing the whole gang to a mask-making workshop, we say: We'll get back to you.

4. Ditziness can be attractive in the young, but the cool parent always phones ahead for details, schedules, admission prices, and directions. The cool parent consults a detailed map before starting out. Then the cool parent brings the map along.

5. The cool parent always carries snacks, knowing that sometimes kids have to eat when they have to eat, and that gnawing hunger can mess up an outing before it's begun.

6. Speaking of food, the cool parent understands that there's more to family dining-out than McDonald's, Wendy's, and the local pizza joint.

7. The cool parent shuns most parades, street fairs, food festivals, and the like for any child under the age of ten. Here's why:

    • Little kids at these functions are routinely stepped on and elbowed.

    • The noise and the crush are so great that you usually can't hear what's wrong when your wailing child tugs at your arm and tries to tell you.

    • Brass bands, bagpipers, and steel drummers terrify them.

    • Nothing could interest a child less than stained-glass doodads and foods of many lands.

8. The cool parent is aware that at regular intervals the kids need to "veg out," that is, to give up on meaningful activity and watch TV or do something equally moronic. Those inclined to guilt can make an enriching experience out of this, such as a Buster Keaton film festival with homemade popcorn and other treats. You could even forget the homemade aspect.

9. The cool parent is an improvisational virtuoso. (Translation: if something isn't working, bag it.)

10. The cool parent knows that discretion is the better part of valor and that in New York City it always pays to keep your eyes open, especially in unfamiliar territory. On the other hand, the cool parent is not a scaredy-cat, even when venturing into terra incognita (say, down a manhole in the middle of Atlantic Avenue, see page 51).

Is this you? Of course it is. As a New York City parent, you're already cooler than most, since New York City is the world's coolest place. You're perennially up for the treasures, excitements, serendipities, and secrets that New York has to offer—except, of course, when it feels like a better day to stay home and lurk, also a very cool thing to do.

How to Use this Book

Like Dr. Scholl's moleskin, these excursions should be trimmed to fit. Many of them include more than you and yours will be able to cover in one day. Our aim is not to exhaust you, but to provide frameworks within which you can create your own itineraries, depending on the ages, interests, and energy levels of your kids.

We live in a rapidly changing world, and nothing changes more often or arbitrarily than business hours. So we've simply provided all the necessary phone numbers. Trust no one but the horse's (or museum's) mouth. **Call ahead first.** (Another good reason to do so is to find out about additional programs and special events. Many of the institutions we recommend offer kid-centric activities worth investigating. So go on, call.)

Subways are faster than buses, which make them easier for kids to manage, so we provide subway directions for the most part and bus routes only where essential. If you prefer to travel by bus, you can get all the information you need by calling 718-330-1234, a Transit Authority help line that is actually, of all things, helpful.

As of this writing, prices for the activities we recommend are moderate, by which we mean they are unlikely to cause more than the usual twitching as you reach for your wallet. When things get a little pricier—as in our Ten Treats (see pages 135-141) for example—we tell you. But prices, as we all know too well, are subject to change, so please don't blame us if (or rather, when) they increase.

We believe strongly that you are the best judge of whether your child is the proper age, gender, and type for the excursions we describe. So, with a few exceptions, we limit ourselves to telling you what there is to do and leave it to you to decide whether it's right for your family.

into the melting pot:

ethnic new york

Familiar Exotica: Chinatown

Strolling, shopping, eating...The new Museum of Chinese in America...weird fish and wondrous jerky...an enduringly tacky arcade...stationery and toys...a Buddhist temple...food, glorious food... a super supermarket for souvenirs.

Here's a partial list of items you can buy on the narrow streets of Chinatown: tiny turtles, huge transformers, Kangol cap knockoffs, a Golden Tai Chi Energy Belt, tabletop shrines, jade flowers, battery-operated hula girls and bathtub scuba divers, back scratchers, ear picks, paper parasols, live eels and, for $178 a pound, dried Japanese sea cucumbers, which are decidedly not vegetables. Is it any wonder that Chinatown is eternally intriguing to children—and to their parents, too?

Loud, bustling, and crowded, Chinatown is a tourist destination that is also an immigrant world with a proud history and an invigorating present. Unfamiliar smells, sights, and sounds are everywhere in this wall-to-wall bazaar of odd merchandise and fabulous food. A walk through its twisty streets is always an adventure.

Start your visit with a painless history lesson at the **Museum of Chinese in America**, a community anchor for more than twenty years, newly installed in a beautiful new home designed by Maya Lin (the architect best known for the Vietnam Veterans Memorial in Washington, D.C.). This museum conjures up, with objects, photographs, and documents, the hard world that Chinese immigrants faced when they came to America. Children will like the colorful dragon and pagoda-shaped phone box; you can show them the eight-pound irons used by laundrymen and the tiny embroidered shoes made to fit bound feet.

Now for a look at what Chinatown has become. When you leave the museum, walk two blocks east to Mulberry where, for a couple of blocks, Chinatown and Little Italy create a model of peaceful coexistence. Cross Canal, heading toward Chatham Square, the heart of the district, but don't rush. Instead, look around. Look at the fish markets, for example. Fish here is inexpensive and very fresh—sometimes still moving, in fact. On our last trip, we saw geoducks (giant clams), crayfish, and mudfish (which look a lot better than they sound). The butchers sell beef shin, pork blood, and duck feet. Dried fish and puzzling vegetables are piled high in grocers' stalls. (Look for a durian, which is a large melon with spikey skin. If it's been cut open, you'll smell it before you see it!) Buy some delicious small mangoes or an unknown leafy green. Notice that the plastic bag is usually red or orange, which symbolizes luck, and almost never white, which symbolizes death.

Just off Mulberry on Bayard Street is **New Beef King**, which offers beef and pork jerky in several flavors, including oyster and spicy. It's made on the premises daily and very tasty, with a chewy mouth-feel similar to fruit leather. Kids will like it, especially the fruit flavor; you might like yours with a cocktail. Down Mulberry is **Columbus Park**, with a splash fountain for the little ones, a playground and basketball hoops. In the morning you'll see ranks of locals doing their stretching exercises and in all weather, men playing table games—backgammon, go, and chess—surrounded by rapt kibitzers. Turn left at the bottom of Mulberry and then left again. This is Mott Street, Chinatown's main artery and reassuring proof that no amount of modernization or gentrification can diminish Chinatown's sublime tackiness.

Nowhere is this more fully realized than at the **Chinatown Fair** at 8 Mott, a dingy arcade packed with vintage and current video games. It's always busy and loud, full of local kids and tourists feeding quarters into their machines in an atmosphere of amiable grime and unsuitability. Your children will love it. Note the words in the center of the well-worn sign outside: "World Famo s [sic] Dancing & Tic-Tac-Toe..." Underneath these words is a barely legible smudge, a ghost of the word that once completed the sign: "Chickens." Gone but not forgotten. Neither, we suspect, will you forget the cover-all-bases name of the eating establishment across the street, the Buddha Bodai Nature Kosher Vegetarian Restaurant.

Back on the street, it's tchotcke heaven. An immaculate shop called **Munchies Paradise** offers tiny candies and more mysterious snacks (dried squid, sesame marshmallows, preserved lemon) in astonishing variety. Free samples abound. **The Chinatown Gift Center** offers an impressive array of Digimon, Pokemon, and Dragonball Z-related comics, videos, and models; there are also holy cows (they have wings attached), flying pigs (ditto), and something called the Trump Force Weapon Play Set. Keep an eye out for the elaborate transformer samurai sold by many newsstands and sidewalk vendors. Each is composed of smaller transformers; they tend to fall apart when handled, but they look great and the packaging has not one word of English on it—very impressive to the right kid.

You can sometimes find tiny turtles for sale in Chinatown, piled in bowls of water in shops or simply on the street. Be warned: It's illegal to sell turtles under four inches in length and all of these are. But if you have the urge to invest in some adorable contraband, it'll cost you less than ten dollars. Of course, that doesn't include the hundred or so dollars worth of gear—tank, filter, light, heater—that you'll have to buy to ensure that your turtle lives longer than a week. Still, the critters make excellent city pets: quiet, well behaved, and smaller than a bichon frisé.

Meander down the side streets. A sign outside the Excellent Pork Chop Restaurant on Doyers Street declares, "Closed Tuesday. Sorry for the Inconvenient." In shop windows on Doyers and Pell, there are mahjong and domino sets, also wonderfully illustrated flash cards for learning English, each drawing accompanied by the appropriate Chinese and English words. For a wider range of novelties, including Chinese checkers, lucky money envelopes, and a book in Chinese about Tibetan Mastiffs, try **Oriental Books and Stationery** at 29 East Broadway. Step into one of the tiny herbalist shops; your childrens' eyes will widen at the heaped ginseng roots, dried fungi, and ominous-looking potions on display.

Chinatown also has a quieter, spiritual side. Among the temples that dot the community, perhaps the most serene is the **Eastern States Buddhist Temple** at 64 Mott Street, with incense burning, bronze Buddhas gleaming in the candlelight and senior citizens lounging in the anteroom.

Finally, the moment of truth: where to eat? On the Bowery, the celebrated **Great New York Noodletown** specializes in homemade guess-what in a no-frills but friendly atmosphere. **The Nom Wah Tea Parlor**, on Doyers Street since 1920, is the oldest teahouse in New York and looks it: well-worn wooden tables, patched red vinyl booths, and ancient fans overhead. Waiters roll carts of dumplings by and you point at what you'd like. The almond cookies are said to be the biggest in Chinatown. For a more modern spin on the same style of food, try **Dim Sum Go Go**, a bright, airy establishment popular with both uptown foodies and local families. Since Chinese food and children are a mutual admiration society, picking where you'll eat can be an activity unto itself, with little risk of grave disappointment. At the worst, someone will end up eating a bun stuffed with crunchy chicken feet.

For dessert, stop into a local bakery like the **Golden Fung Wong** for a cookie or a honey bow, which looks like an enormous fried noodle dipped in honey. Try a cooling "bubble tea," sweetened tea with milk and chewy tapioca pearls in flavors both tempting (watermelon, blueberry) and curious (avocado, taro). **Tea-riffic** and **Vivi Bubble Tea** are both clearly popular with local kids. The **Chinatown Ice Cream Factory** makes 36 homemade flavors, including green tea and pineapple. This shop also sells a bright yellow T-shirt depicting a dragon eating a cone; it's a winner.

Finish up with a souvenir for yourself. At **Kam Man Food Products** on Canal, the pace is less hectic than on the street, the range of merchandise is incredible, and the prices are low. Along with dozens of varieties of soy sauce and dried fish big as your leg (or small as your finger), Kam Man also sells cookware, cutlery, and serving dishes. Most importantly, it is one of the only places we have found that sells plastic sushi of respectable quality.

- **Museum of Chinese in America**, *211–215 Centre St. bet. Howard and Grand Sts., 212-619-4785, www.mocanyc.org. Note: On Saturdays, the museum sponsors walking tours and, for families, living arts work-*

shops, which vary in theme. Call to find out more or reserve a place.

- **Chinatown Fair**, 8 Mott St. bet. Park Row and Pell St.
- **Oriental Books and Stationery**, 29 E. Broadway bet. Catherine and Market Sts., 212-962-3634.
- **Eastern States Buddhist Temple of America**, 64 Mott St. bet. Bayard and Canal Sts., 212-966-6229 (there is no English lettering on the sign, so look carefully).
- **Munchies Paradise**, 37 Mott St. at Pell St., 212-233-7650, www.ajiichiban-usa.com. Note: Munchies Paradise has branches at 23 E. Broadway, 167 Hester St., 188 Lafayette St., and 153A Centre St.
- **New Beef King**, 89 Bayard St. at Mulberry St. 212-233-6612, www.newbeefking.com.
- **Great New York Noodletown**, 28 1/2 Bowery at Doyers St., 212-349-0923.
- **Nom Wah Tea Parlor**, 13 Doyers St. at Bowery, 212-226-3553.
- **Dim Sum Go Go**, 5 E. Broadway bet. Catherine St. and Bowery, 212-732-0796.
- **Chinatown Ice Cream Factory**, 65 Bayard St. bet. Mott and Elizabeth Sts., 212-608-4170, www.chinatownice-creamfactory.com.
- **Golden Fung Wong**, 41 Mott St. bet. Pell and Bayard Sts., 212-267-4037.
- **Kam Man Food Products**, 200 Canal St. bet. Mulberry and Mott Sts., 212-962-8414
- **Tea-riffic**, 51 Mott St. at Bayard St., 212-393-9009.
- **Vivi Bubble Tea**, 49 Bayard St at Elizabeth St., 212-566-6833.
- **Getting there:** Subway: 6, N, R, Q, W, J, M and Z to Canal St.; B and D to Grand St.

A View of Old Manhattoes: Inwood Hill Park

Where original Americans lived and newer Americans play...Indian caves...intense baseball...Dyckman Farmhouse Museum...best carrot cake ever.

At some point in their lives, Manhattanites—even small ones—wonder what their island looked like before developers started messing it up. The best surviving glimpse of that distant past is at Manhattan's northernmost tip, where Inwood Hill Park contains, among its nearly two-hundred acres, the largest natural woodlands on the island. Wear your climbing clothes for this one.

Enter the park via Isham Park on Isham Street, passing the playing fields on your right; then bear to the right as the path diverges. Soon the foliage thickens, the walkway narrows and begins to climb, and the woods seem to loom: hickory, hackberry, yellow poplar, birch, sweetgum, spicebush (the twigs of which Native Americans used as chewing gum), and beautiful quaking aspen, whose leaves rustle and shimmer in the breeze.

Keep going until you see steep, rocky outcroppings up the hill on your left. The caves created by these overhanging ledges of rock were once inhabited by Indians. Time to leave the path; this climb is steep and requires some care, especially if the ground is wet. But it's not Everest, and in exchange for some huffing and puffing, you'll find deep, secluded niches in the rocks where the children can hunker down and you can remove yourself from the sights and sounds of the city. You may even see a shrew or vole, those pleasantly rustic relatives of New York's commoner rodents.

Once atop the cliffs, find the path that leads toward the Hudson River. The great view is even greater if you slip between the gaps in the chicken-wire fencing on the path's river side. When you come back down, pass the caves and go back down onto the original path. Continue ahead until you come to a plaque where Peter Minuit's purchase of Manhattan Island from the Canarsie Indians was supposedly consummated. (In these leafy surroundings you can believe it, although historians say the deal was more likely closed at the Battery, where the Dutch had settled.)

Make sure to visit the **Inwood Hill Nature Center**, operated by the Urban Park Rangers and housed in an old Columbia University boathouse. This friendly, busy place is action central for Park Ranger doings in northern Manhattan. Call ahead or get on the mailing list for advance word of its many activities.

During the week, it's full of kids on school trips; weekends are devoted to lectures and hikes that families can do together. The rangers can point out fragments of wall scattered in the underbrush where lavish homes (including that of Samuel Lord of Lord & Taylor) and a Revolutionary War-era fort once stood. They can show you where to gather nettles for soup or point out species of non-native trees, like copper beeches, that were planted by settlers and have flourished here. During the season, there are canoe programs, planting and conservation projects, and a Winterfest. At least once a year, the Manhattan and Bronx Rangers collaborate on the **Manhattan to Bronx Connection**, a guided hike around the Park, over the Henry Hudson Bridge and back.

At the top end of the park you'll see the turbulent Spuyten Duyvil, where the Hudson and Harlem rivers meet, not amicably. You are at the very tip of Manhattan island. Rowers in sculls from the Columbia boathouse glide by and, weather permitting, some of the most exciting baseball in New York takes place on the diamonds up here. The teams are largely Dominican, and their game is skilled, hard-hitting, and ferociously competitive. Stand behind the batting cage, watching fastballs whiz by and waiting for the crack of ball on bat. It's a lot more thrilling than watching a game on TV.

Afterwards, head downtown to the **Dyckman Farmhouse Museum** on Broadway, Manhattan's only surviving Dutch Colonial farmhouse. Built in 1784 and once the hub of a 450-acre spread, it has been painstakingly restored to its original condition and appears at first like a hallucination: a rustic antiquity on a completely urban street. Many of the objects on display belonged to the Dyckman family—though probably not the munitions, uniforms, and Hessian crockery you'll find in the Relic Room. The kitchen has great, sturdy cooking implements next to the open hearth. Right outside the kitchen window, scratched into the big stone outcropping, is a playing board for Nine Man Morris, an eighteenth-century children's game.

204th Street is bustling, so food isn't hard to find. Diagonally across the street from the Dyckman Farmhouse is a Dunkin' Donuts. A few blocks up Broadway is **Carrot Top**

Pastries, whose renowned carrot cake is, according to Molly O'Neill's *New York Cookbook*, the best in the world. This little pastry shop has a few tables and a small selection of sandwiches, quiches, and soups besides the home-baked goods. (We love the hot apple pie.) If you prefer, look for one of the many comfy Cuban-Chinese restaurants nearby, where children are welcome and can be made very happy with rice and beans, fried bananas, chicken and rice, and other not-too-spicy favorites. Remember, these Cuban-Chinese joints serve beer and wine, so pop a Corona and relax. The subway ride back home is always faster.

- **Inwood Hill Park**, *between Dyckman St., the Hudson River, and the Harlem River Ship Canal, www.nycgovparks.org. The Isham Park entrance is on Isham St., one block north of 207th St. and west of Broadway.*
- **Inwood Hill Nature Center**, *218th St. and Indian Rd., 212–628-2345 (call to receive a copy of their calendar of events).*
- **Dyckman Farmhouse Museum**, *4881 Broadway at 204th St., 212-304-9422, www.dyckmanfarmhouse.org.*
- **Carrot Top Pastries**, *5025 Broadway at 214th St., 212-569-1532, www.carrottoppastries.com.*
- **Getting there:** *Subway: A train to 207th St. or 1 to 215th St.*

Downtown, Back When: Lower East Side and Environs
The Lower East Side Tenement Museum...Strolling Orchard and Essex...St. Augustine's Episcopal Church...Eldridge Street Synagogue...Love Saves the Day...Trash & Vaudeville...at long last, dinner.

When your kids are old enough to be genuinely curious about the ways New Yorkers lived in other times, take a trip to the Lower East Side, former home to successive waves of immigrants from Ireland, Germany, Eastern Europe, Latin America, and Asia. Despite the rising tide of hipness sweeping the area, traces of that immigrant past still resonate here, nowhere more powerfully than at the **Lower East Side Tenement Museum** on Orchard Street. This is a very popular place; book tickets in advance and pick them up at the Visitors' Center and Gift Shop at 108 Orchard Street, just below Delancey.

Arrive early enough to watch the free video produced for the museum by the History Channel. It's twenty-five minutes long and provides easily digested background and context for what you're about to see across the street in the museum itself, at 97 Orchard. Several different tours are offered, each visiting two of the three restored apartments in the building, painstakingly recreated to convey the lives of the families who actually lived there between the 1870s and the 1930s. (A fourth, once inhabited by the Moores, an Irish family, opens in 2008.) Keep in mind that the building has neither heat nor air conditioning, so dress accordingly. In hot weather, fans and water are provided.

At the entrance, a guide leads you up the stoop and into a pitch-black hallway. This is how it was for generations of the building's tenants. An electric light, a twentieth-century addition, comes on and you're in a deep, narrow space with dingy, custard-colored walls lined with doors, and a steep staircase to the apartments above. It's claustrophobic; it feels depressing and slum-like to twenty-first-century New Yorkers, but the guide gently reminds you that when this place was built in 1863, it was considered a desirable place to live. No.97 reeks of history.

There's a wonderful special feature for families—a 45-minute visit to the Confino apartment, led by a guide costumed as fourteen-year-old Victoria Confino. The Confinos, a family of Sephardic Jews, arrived from Turkey in 1916. Victoria greets you as if you've just gotten off the boat yourself, proudly showing you around the place and filling you in on what awaits you in New York. Kids will be astonished to talk to this charming, vivacious girl who doesn't know what television is, but is ecstatic to have a flushing toilet instead of an outdoor privy. Victoria gets them to wind up the Victrola and handle such implements as the "washer agitator." If you're up for it, she'll teach you the foxtrot. All along, she's talking about immigrant life on the Lower East Side—schools, jobs, health, nickel movies at the nickelodeon, and who sleeps where when ten people share a one-bedroom apartment. It's riveting to hear all this "firsthand." Everything about this museum is engaging, from its website (where you can click on a little square of wallpaper to reveal the layer beneath, click again to find the next layer down, and so on) to its volunteers, some of whom are old folks who remember how it used to be and some of whom are recent arrivals. All seem to delight in sharing their memories and impressions.

Afterwards, make a pit stop at **Il Laboratorio del Gelato** for ice cream that's hand-made and intensely flavored, though not quite as intensely as the delicacies to be found just down the block at **Guss' Pickles**, the last word in Kosher pickles, made in the Bronx according to recipes known only to the owner. Full-sours are brined for ten months; they are celestial, whatever the kids think.

After you've been perked up by a sweet or sour snack, it's time to stroll, keeping in mind that on a Saturday most of the Jewish businesses will be closed. The storefronts on Orchard and Essex Streets illustrate the cultural mix that thrives here: zoot suits in thirteen colors at the New Era Factory Outlet, art at the Miguel Abreu Gallery, remedies at the Quan Herb Shop and guess what? at Orchard Sausages. A mostly Hebrew sign over the window at 17 Essex announces Ha-Attikos Judaica, but a look in the window reveals a bronze Buddha and racks of dry-cleaning. Further on are Frank's Chop Shop (hip haircuts) and Main Squeeze ("for all your accordion needs"). Look closely in the cluttered window of Mendel Weissberg's Religious Articles (45 Essex) and you'll find small wooden figures of Groucho Marx, the Three Stooges, Charlie Chaplin, and Abbot and Costello.

Head south to **St. Augustine's Episcopal Church** on Henry Street, which was built in the 1820s. If you call ahead, you may be able to arrange a look at the church's claustrophobic little gallery overlooking the nave, where slaves were permitted to worship. They were immigrants too, albeit unwilling ones (and they were traded downtown, at Pearl and Wall Streets). You can also walk west to the **Eldridge Street Synagogue**, newly and splendidly restored after decades of neglect. Built in 1887, its sumptuous stained glass windows, terracotta facade, elaborate masonry and Depression-era stenciling and murals are back in all their glory. Call or look online for visiting hours and tour schedules.

If you go north to Houston Street, you can line up at **Katz's** for enormous deli sandwiches or crisp franks. A mere knish's throw away there's **Pomme-Pomme**, where Belgian fries come with a variety of sauces, including ketchup. Take home some edible memories from **Streit's Matzos**, where the baking is done behind the counter, as it has been since 1925 or from **Economy Candy**, with its chocolate band-aids, bubble gum cigars, and other sweets that time forgot.

There's a newer, more light-hearted brand of nostalgia a little bit uptown in New York's kitsch 'n' camp headquarters, the East Village. The venerable (since 1966) **Love Saves the Day** is impossibly cluttered with Davy Crockett hats, collectible toys, and vintage lunchboxes; **Trash and Vaudeville** has tiny tube skirts from England, skinny jeans, and magenta feather boas for budding fashionistas.

Remember, stuff that looks this cheap seldom is; these places can be pricey. Shrug it off, splurge and gloat over your purchases at a casual East Village restaurant like **Telephone Bar & Grill**, which has a jolly red English phone box outside, kidpleasing bangers and mash or fish and chips inside. Trusty **Two Boots** is there too, with its festive, tinselly decor, its combination Italian/Louisiana cooking (which actually works, especially the pizza) and a patient and forgiving wait staff that extends itself to make children feel at home. Sit down, cocktail in hand, and know that you've been good parents.

- **Lower East Side Tenement Museum**, *108 Orchard St. bet. Delancey and Broome, 212-431-0233, www.tenement.org. Note: Within the next two years or so, the Visitors' Center will be moving across the street to 103 Orchard St.*
- **Il Laboratorio del Gelato**, *95 Orchard St. bet. Delancey and Broome Sts., 212-343-9922, www.laboratoriodelgelato.com.*

- **Guss' Pickles**, *87 Orchard St. bet. Broome and Grand Sts., 212-334-3616.*
- **St. Augustine's Church**, *290 Henry St., one block east of Chatham Sq.*
- **Eldridge Street Synagogue**, *12 Eldridge St. bet. Canal and Division, 212-219-0888, www.eldridgestreet.org.*
- **Katz's Delicatessen**, *205 East Houston St. at Ludlow St., 212-254-2246, www.katzdeli.com.*
- **Pomme-Pomme**, *191 East Houston St. bet. Ludlow and Orchard Sts., 646-602-8140.*
- **Streit's Matzos**, *150 Rivington St. bet. Essex and Norfolk Sts., 212-475-7000, www.streitsmatzos.com.*
- **Economy Candy**, *108 Rivington St. bet. Essex and Ludlow Sts., 800-352-4544, www.economycandy.com.*
- **Love Saves the Day**, *119 Second Ave. at 7th St., 212-228-3802.*
- **Trash & Vaudeville**, *4 St. Marks Pl. bet. Second and Third Aves., 212-982-3590, www.nycgoth.com.*
- **Telephone Bar & Grill,** *149 Second Ave. bet. E. 9th and E. 10th Sts., 212-529-5000, www.telebar.com.*
- **Two Boots**, *37 Avenue A bet. 2nd and 3rd Sts., 212-505-2276, www.twoboots.com.*
- **Getting there:** *F train to Delancey St., B, D, or Q to Grand St., J, M, or Z train to Essex St.*

museums
without pain

Ten Tips for Visiting Museums

Even among New Yorkers, for whom cultural treasures are an everyday fact of life, it is widely felt that museums and children don't mix, except during school trips. At the mention of a family museum trip, many parents roll their eyes or make jokes about dragging the kids along in handcuffs. We feel their pain but beg to differ. Here are some pointers:

1. **Just Do It**: Make your own plan before going. Consulting with the kids will only muddy the waters. Once there, stride firmly toward your choices. Of course, if they clamor to look at something, take them right over.

2. **Prime Them**: Make sure they know something about immigrants if you're going to the Tenement Museum. They'll feel better about going, and they'll get more out of it.

3. **Be Brief**: Focus on the things you've picked or the things that tickle them, and then get out of there in no more than an hour.

4. **Tourist Class**: For some museums, it's really helpful to take an organized tour or use the audio. A portrait that looks like just another gloomy face might have an interesting or creepy story behind it or a noteworthy squirrel in the background. But if the tour guide isn't keeping your kids' attention, have the courage to walk away!

5. **Art, Schmart**: Kids aren't scared of art and will approach whatever you put in front of them with a fresh, questioning gaze. One caveat, though: The Old Masters, with their classical themes, murky backgrounds, and big-boned naked ladies, tend to turn kids off. So wait a while for Rembrandt and Rubens.

6. **Gimmicks Work**: Always have a few up your sleeve. In a room full of artifacts or paintings, split up and each take a side. Then meet up, report which was the best thing and why, and switch sides. (Make sure you're listening as much as talking.) Or play a game, such as I Spy.

7. **Your Gifted Child:** If your child begins to pout and fret before you've even gone inside, head immediately for the

gift shop and collaborate in picking out the nicest post-cards. Then make it your mission to go looking for the originals.

8. **Feed the Body, Then the Soul**: To head off pouting and fretting, make sure that no one's hungry at the start.

9. **Phone First**: See if there are any special programs or events that day. Also check to see whether the museum has a treasure hunt/discovery sheet/special activity booklet for kids. The thrill of the chase makes everything more interesting. (Armed with a quiz, our son once got briefly interested in some rusty old farm implements in an English village museum.)

10. **Bribe 'Em**: Set a price limit, and let them choose. Someday they'll grow out of that need to buy something, anything; but probably not today.

Brooklyn's (Cultural) Heights
**Brooklyn Museum...Brooklyn Botanic Garden...
Tom's Restaurant... Soldiers and Sailors Arch.**

If the **Brooklyn Museum** were anywhere else in the country, it would be perpetually packed. Its world-class collection is the second largest in the country, and the building is a grand, looming Beaux Arts pile in front of which a flying saucer seems to have landed.

The extraordinary entrance, all glass, brushed steel, and stone, was completed in 2004 and returns grandeur to the building, whose front staircase was amputated in 1936. Outside are spacious seating areas and a delightful "dancing" fountain that shoots jets of water skywards. Kids love to run along the walkway that follows the curve of the stepped glass entrance pavilion. It's weird, but it works.

The museum has its own subway stop and a parking lot of respectable size (presided over by a squat but dignified replica of the Statue of Liberty). And it's next door to the superb **Brooklyn Botanic Garden**. Even with all this going for it, the museum is rarely crowded—except on the first Saturday night of each month, when admission is free, and there are special events. On a weekend afternoon, it's a great place to visit.

Start on the fifth floor in the American Identities exhibit. It's very kid-friendly, the art augmented by videos and comments posted by children about specific works. One of the first works you encounter is Francis Guy's *Winter Scene in Brooklyn*, in which every person is modeled from life. Painted in 1820, it seems as reliable a record as a photo. Two portraits of George Washington gaze out side by side, one of them depicting a much younger man than we're used to seeing. The beautiful pastoral landscapes by Thomas Cole and William Sidney Mount are full of fascinating details and heartfelt affection for their subjects. Your child will not believe that the shiny aluminum victrola from 1935 is called "portable;" it's as big as a suitcase. Next to Louis Remy Mignot's *Niagara* is a comment posted by a seventh grader: "This is a beautiful picture."

Also on this floor is something most unusual, the Visible Storage Study Center, where 2000 objects not on exhibit at the moment are stored neatly—but very compactly—in glass cases. There are six hundred paintings here in rolling racks. Each object is identified only by a number, which you can enter into one of several computer stations to obtain information about the work. It's like getting a peek backstage.

On the fourth floor, the memorial panel by Walter Cole Brigham is the most fabulous of the stained-glass panels on view; it's made of chunks of glass as thick as jewels. The atmospheric period rooms allow kids to peer into the past. Search out the Victorian parlor with a long double line of small wooden animals winding across the floor to Noah's Ark.

The high point of the Egyptian collection on the third floor has got to be the mummy—it's real! Theres also a wonderful gold ibis which has become the museum's unofficial mascot. Then it's down to the ground floor with its towering totem poles, spooky masks, and New World artifacts. The well-stocked gift shop is here, as well as the learning center where, on weekends, four to seven-year-olds and their parents can join Arty Facts, a drop-in art program (call for times).

There's a decent cafeteria on the first floor, but we suggest you head straight across Eastern Parkway and down

Washington Avenue to **Tom's Restaurant**, an old-fashioned luncheonette festooned with artificial flowers and signs touting cherry lime rickeys, egg creams, and banana-walnut pancakes. Everyone's friendly (especially owner Gus Vlahadas, who has been called "the friendliest man in Brooklyn"); the burgers are manageable for small hands, the fries are crisp, and the egg salad not too mayonnaise-y. It's not only the children who'll feel welcome.

You could also walk through the parking lot and into the **Brooklyn Botanic Garden** for good chili, sandwiches, and ice-cream, and then take in the conservatory greenhouses. Each of the four is a different little world with its own climate—in the rainforest, kids will get a kick out of the perpetual drips and towering banana tree with its drooping load of fruit. In the desert, the motley array of cacti is stunning.

The Japanese Garden is not just serene and beautiful; it has turtles, ducks, and giant carp to feed (the ducks prefer whole wheat bread). Keep an eye peeled for the truly enormous turtle, which from time to time ominously looms up from the depths—the biggest critter in the pond by a wide margin. Stroll down the path by the pond. Head away from the Japanese Garden and soon you'll come to a steep, stone-lined alcove off to the side. While the smallest members fling themselves around this rocky redoubt, you can catch your breath and admire the scenery. If you're lucky, a heron will glide overhead to its nest in a tree by the pond.

When its thousands of varieties are blooming, the Rose Garden can make even the youngest jaw drop. Call for information about the Cherry Blossom Festival, which offers not just acres of blooms, but Japanese music, dancing, and impressive martial arts demonstrations.

The museum and botanic gardens are a short walk away from Grand Army Plaza. On select days in spring or fall, you can climb the hundred or so steps to the top of the **Soldiers and Sailors Arch** for a spectacular view of Prospect Park, the harbor, and the city; or you can linger at ground level to watch newly-weds stepping out of white limos to be photographed in front of the fountains.

- **Brooklyn Museum**, *200 Eastern Pkwy. at Washington Ave., 718-638-5000, www.brooklynmuseum.org.*
- **Brooklyn Botanic Garden**, *1000 Washington Ave., 718-623-7200, www.bbg.org.*
- **Tom's Restaurant**, *782 Washington Ave. at Sterling Pl., 718-636-9738.*
- **Soldiers and Sailors Arch at Grand Army Plaza**, *Prospect Park Alliance, 718-965-8951.*
- **Getting there:** *2 or 3 to Eastern Pkwy-Brooklyn Museum (East Siders, take the 4 or 5 train to Nevins St., then walk across the platform to transfer to the 2 or 3).*

Queens of Arts (and Sciences)
Flushing Meadows, indoors and out...Unisphere...Queens Museum of Art...Panorama of the City of New York...Hall of Science...serious barbecue.

Flushing Meadows in Queens has many delights, both indoors and out, and you can reach them without the hassle of driving. It's positively liberating to find yourself in such a wide and grassy space after stepping off the subway. There are enough things to do for a couple of trips. If you're heading here for the first time, you've got choices to make.

This is, of course, the place where two celebrated Worlds' Fairs were held. Checking on their remains has the thrill of an archaeological dig for adults, while the scale of the surviving structures alone will make the kids giddy and exultant. You won't be able to stop them from racing toward the gigantic **Unisphere**—which you've undoubtedly seen many times from the accursed L.I.E. (isn't it nice to be looking the other way?)—so follow along and prepare to be amazed. You are looking at the largest globe in the world. Made for the '64 Fair, the spherical grid with steel plates for continents is 140 feet high and weighs 700,000 pounds. In the summer, fountains play around it. Prepare for much frolicking on the steps around the pool; bring skates or skateboards and the camera.

The Unisphere sits right in front of the **Queens Museum of Art**, whose building is the only surviving remnant of the 1939

Worlds' Fair and was the original home of the United Nations. Today, it's home to the **Panorama of the City of New York**, an architectural scale model of the whole city. It contains upwards of 895,000 tiny buildings as well as highways, bridges, and other landmarks. You can walk around the edge of the whole area on a glass-bottomed ramp built a few feet above it. The room is subdued, with people pointing and peering, trying to find where they live. At regular intervals, a little plane takes off from LaGuardia, the sky darkens, and light gleams from within the houses as night falls. A visit to the Panorama is a heady experience, especially for kids—for once, they're bigger than anything in the city. Don't forget to bring binoculars, which make it much easier to search for your building.

Across Grand Central Parkway, within easy walking distance over a little bridge, is the **New York Hall of Science**, another wondrous '64 relic (with additions) built in the shape of an undulating curtain. This place is a welcome antidote to the hi-tech flash of other science centers; there's no glitz to bombard you, no big crowds to distract. Instead, here's a low-key and peaceful hands-on museum, which gives children umpteen scientific tricks to do. If they're old enough, they can learn from them; if they're really young, they'll just have a great time playing. There's a 3-D model of a molecule and a 400-pound pendulum whose swing you can alter with magnets. Time your fastball, measure how high you can leap, observe bacteria through a microscope, arm wrestle over the Internet, and walk through the (enlarged) eye of a needle. There's as much opportunity to move as there is to sit, and the friendly young staff are well able to pull a shy youngster into the swim.

Outside in the Science Playground, the largest of its kind in the country, you can climb a steel-reinforced rope web, experiment with leverage on a giant seesaw, bounce your voice, make water climb and cascade. The playground is open to kids of all ages (adult supervision required) and there's a nominal extra charge to get in. The excellent gift shop features an inexpensive "starter" microscope; the inevitable astronaut ice cream is (and kids will concur) disgusting enough to put you right off space travel. The cafe is adequate, but we suggest holding out.

Next door there's the compact and appealing **Queens Zoo**. Its focus is on animals of the Americas and it has impressive South American spectacled bears, immense bison and elk, and a geodesic-domed aviary (designed by Buckminster Fuller himself for the '64 Fair) in which hawks, turkeys, and gaudy green monk parakeets, among other species, soar, strut, and perch. The sweet petting zoo has the usual farmyard atmosphere and animals (also llamas!). Nearby is the **Playground for All Children**, whose equipment and layout have been sensitively designed to accommodate kids with special physical needs.

Someone is surely ready to eat by now. Fortunately, you're only two blocks from the **Lemon Ice King of Corona**, a chrome-clad classic that always has twenty-odd (some very odd) flavors on hand, including peanut butter and chocolate. Nothing's better on a hot day.

Save room, however, for another of Queens' culinary delights, just a few stops away on the 7 train, where **Ranger Texas Barbecue**, a direct descendent of the immortal Pearson's and Stick to Your Ribs, serves the best BBQ in New York. Located in the back of **Legends Sports Bar**, the decidedly casual Ranger consists of a handful of wooden tables where you can chomp blissfully on fragrant trays of meat brought from the wood burning pit outside while staring absently at sports on TV. You dine off paper plates, and the food—brisket, ribs, chicken, chopped pork on sweet Portuguese rolls, outstanding fries and beans, coleslaw, cobblers, and brownies—is sublime.

- **Unisphere and Queens Museum of Art**, *Flushing Meadows-Corona Park, Queens, 718-592-9700, www.queensmuseum.org.*
- **New York Hall of Science**, *47–01 111th St., Flushing Meadows Corona Park, Queens, 718-699-0005, www.nyscience.org.*
- **Queens Zoo and Playground for All Children**, *Flushing Meadows Corona Park, Queens, 718-271-1500, www.nyzoosandaquarium.com/qz.*
- **Lemon Ice King of Corona**, *52-02 108th St. at 52nd Ave., Queens, 718-699-5133.*

- **Ranger Texas Barbecue at Legends Sports Bar**, *71–04 35th Ave. at 71st St., Queens, 718-779-6948.*
- **Getting there:** *To get to Flushing Meadows, take the No. 7 train from Times Square to Willets Point/Shea Stadium. To get to Pearson's, take the 7 back toward Manhattan to 74th St. and Broadway or the E, F, G, or R to Broadway and Roosevelt Ave. (it's the same stop).*

Naval Engagements
The Harbor Defense Museum at Fort Hamilton...homemade ice cream in Bay Ridge...Intrepid anticipation...cupcakes.

There are military bases on either end of the Verrazano-Narrows Bridge, but only the one on the Brooklyn side is still active. That's Fort Hamilton, an Army base that dates back to 1825. Here, you'll find the small but fascinating **Harbor Defense Museum**. It's the only Army museum in the city, and it's housed in a little stone bunker called a *caponier*, which is French for "chicken coop." It contains dioramas of naval battles, ship's models, and antique weapons. Its location is as impressive to children as the collection. Jeeps, cannons, and people in uniform are everywhere, guaranteed to keep young heads swiveling. Call before coming to find out when the free guided tours start. And remember: You are visiting a military base. A valid photo ID is required to enter.

Before getting back on the subway, head over to **Hinsch's** in Bay Ridge, an old-fashioned coffee shop of the kind they aren't making anymore. It's bright and welcoming, and the waitresses are likely to call you "sweetie." Hinsch's does all the classics well: tuna salad, open turkey sandwich, rice pudding. But it's the ice cream you're after. It's made on the premises and is truly something special. Many of the regulars are retired ladies munching egg salad sandwiches, cups of soup, and little dishes of butter pecan, so decorum is expected. But you can oblige—for the sake of the homemade ice cream, which is so good that conversation dwindles away when it's served.

As of this writing, the awe-inspiring **Intrepid**, the immense aircraft carrier, which served in the Second World War and

Vietnam before becoming the **Intrepid Sea Air Space Museum**, is still in dry dock in Staten Island, undergoing renovation and repair. It is scheduled to return to its berth at Pier 86 on West 46th Street on November 11, 2008—Veterans' Day. We hope our favorite exhibits will still be on board, but in any case, visits to this vessel and the others that comprise the museum make for a thrilling outing.

On the carrier's hangar deck, ancient planes and battered space capsules dangle from the ceiling and there is a genuine fighter-plane cockpit that kids can sit in; actually, it's hard to imagine how anyone larger than a child could fit inside. The elaborate table models of some of the Intrepid's World War II engagements are fascinating—a Japanese airplane smaller than your pinkie attempts to escape the great ship, but it trails a wispy cloud of cotton smoke, indicating it's been hit. There's a bathosphere and a gizmo that rotates passengers upside down and sideways simultaneously. This may be how astronauts train, but not right after lunch.

Find the plaque marking the spot where a kamikaze plane hit the ship during World War II, killing thirty-odd crewmen. When you get to the words "You are standing on hallowed ground," the gravity of the place will touch you.

On the wide, breezy flight deck you should be able to see an array of planes and helicopters (including the Concorde). These are the real thing, so if your children should remark that the lethal-looking Blackbird reminds them of *Star Wars*, point out that it is in fact the fastest plane in the world.

Before leaving the carrier, walk to the end of the deck and look north. You can see the Little Red Lighthouse (a rare shore view) nestled under the New York pier of the George Washington Bridge (see p. 54). If it's a weekend between April and October, you might find yourself smiling at pleasure-seekers in life jackets, gamely practicing a lifeboat drill as their cruise ship prepares to embark from the passenger ship terminals next door.

If you're over six and/or can still fit through the small hatchway at its entrance, join the line to enter the Growler, the only guided-missile submarine in the world that's open to the public. This claustrophobic vessel can only accommodate seventeen reasonably lean and limber visitors at a time.

There are tons of restaurants between the pier and the subway, but you might seek out the cute and funky **Cupcake Café**. It's been around for eighteen years—you'll never guess what it's famous for.

- **Harbor Defense Museum of Fort Hamilton**, *230 Sheridan Loop, Fort Hamilton Military Community, Brooklyn, 718-630-4349, www.harbordefensemuseum.com.*
- **Hinsch's Confectionery**, *8518 Fifth Ave. at 86th St., 718-748-2854.*
- **Getting there:** *R train to 95th St./Fourth Ave. Walk down Fourth Ave. and make a left onto 101st St. and proceed one block to main entrance. To shorten the walk, when you exit the subway, take a B16 or B37 bus to Fourth Ave. and 100th St., or the B63 to Fourth Ave. and Shore Rd.*
- **Intrepid Sea Air Space Museum**, *W. 46th St. and Twelfth Ave., 212-245-0072, www.intrepidmuseum.org.*
- **Cupcake Café**, *545 Ninth Ave. at 40th St., 212-465-1530.*
- **Getting there:** *From the nearest subway stop at 42nd St. and Eighth Ave., you still have to walk four blocks north and four long blocks west. However, the M 50 bus stops right at the Intrepid.*

Battle of the (Modernist) Titans: Guggenheim vs. Whitney

Both of these grand Upper East Side institutions offer fine collections in manageable dosages, so they're well suited for young concentration spans. Each trip makes for an interesting outing, but which will be more rewarding? That is the question. And here is the answer:

Location, location, location

The Whitney's closer to the subway, but the Guggenheim's

closer to the park and, if you've got the appetite for it, another short-and-sweet museum—**The Museum of the City of
New York**, which is only a few blocks away and has some
extraordinary old doll houses and toys.
Advantage: Guggenheim.

The Venue

While some question the Guggenheim's merits as an exhibition
space, no one can deny that it's a great playground. More than
one child has been known to compare the main tower to a
gigantic toilet bowl; the giggles begin at that point. Inside, the
space inspires action. Children race up and down the sloped
floors and shout across the cavernous spiral. Be prepared for
the art to be upstaged by stairway landings good for hiding. If
you want your kids to look properly at the exhibits, don't start
at the top of the ramp, which presents them with an irresistible
downward slope. Instead, conduct your tour in a stately way,
uphill.

The Whitney, on the other hand, is an interesting building
if you like that sort of thing, but no one will ever mistake it for
a toilet bowl. The ticket line is chronically slow and the single
elevator, albeit large, creates minor annoyances.
Advantage: Guggenheim again.

The Staff

The Guggenheim often teems with throngs of kids, and
inevitably some of them run, shout, and, of course, try to touch
the art, especially if the art is a big, soft, fabric slice of pie,
which it might be. Perhaps that's why guards and clerks at the
Guggenheim project a quality of having seen everything a
museum guard can possibly see—nothing fazes them. As long
as you don't touch the art, they are pleasant and helpful.

Whitney guards are cool and a little pushy, always realign-
ing the omnipresent ticket queue. It must come from working
on Madison Avenue.
Advantage: Guggenheim.

The Food

The Guggenheim's cafeteria is small, but pleasantly decorated with the sort of swooping lines and curvy chairs you see on *The Jetsons*. It serves modest and unexceptional cafeteria food at the usual museum markup. The Whitney's food service is a branch of Sarabeth's. It's good but pricey, and the menu is not necessarily to a small person's taste.

Advantage: Whitney has better food, Guggenheim has the decor. Neither is really to our taste. Draw.

The Gift Shops

Both offer standard museum merchandise: lovely art books, prints, cards, ties, etc., and tasteful toys that won't get as much use as their prices demand.

Advantage: Draw.

The Art

By far the most important exhibit at the Guggenheim is Frank Lloyd Wright's—that is, the building itself. Beyond that, the Chagalls usually make an impact on kids, reminding them of dreams and fairy tales.

Like the Guggenheim, most of the Whitney's exhibition space is given over to temporary shows, and its permanent collection is frequently rotated, so it's hard to say what will be on display at any moment. However, you can usually count on seeing a couple of Calder mobiles, which children usually love, and some Hoppers, O'Keeffes, and Warhols.

Advantage: Ours is not to evaluate the art of these museums, only to suggest that the Whitney makes it easier for a young person to focus on the art, so the Whitney wins this one.

Final Score: Guggenheim: 3, Whitney: 1, Draws: 2.

Conclusion: You'll probably go to both, but why not start with the Guggenheim? If it goes horribly wrong, you're closer to the park than the toy stores.

- **Solomon R. Guggenheim Museum**, *1071 Fifth Ave. at 89th St., 212-423-3500, www.guggenheim.org.*
- **Museum of the City of New York**, *Fifth Ave. at 103rd St., 212-534-1672, www.mcny.org.*
- **The Whitney Museum of American Art**, *945 Madison Ave. at 75th St., 1-800-WHITNEY, www.whitney.org.*
- **Getting there:** *For the Guggenheim, the 4, 5, or 6 train to 86th St., For the Whitney, the 6 train to 77th St.*

Easy Pieces: Manageable Masterpieces at the Museum of Modern Art

There's something about MoMA's layout—spacious, bright and, well, *modern*—that makes wandering around it feel almost carefree. The best approach is to be selective. The museum recommends spending around thirty minutes there with little ones, and no more than ninety with older children, which means that you need to think expediently. In other words, go for Miro and Magritte over Matisse; pop art over photography.

Our suggested approach: travel chronologically down from the fifth floor to four and three, heading straight for the world-famous masterpieces. After all, they're world-famous for a reason. The fifth floor is home to galleries 1 through 14; up here (in gallery 1) you'll find Van Gogh's *Starry Night* and the glorious velvety textures of Rousseau's *Sleeping Gypsy*. Most New York children have seen a reproduction of Munch's *The Scream* somewhere, even if only on a cushion; they'll feel a shiver of apprehension when they look at his painting *The Storm*. There are oodles of Picassos; we think the kids will like his early works best, particularly the Cubist paintings which have that jigsaw quality to puzzle over (Where's the lady's nose? Her eyes are *there*?). Monet's *Waterlilies* is in gallery 9; the sheer size should impress. You can't miss with galleries 10 through 12, which have Mondrian, Dali, and the aforementioned Miro and Magritte. Miro is especially irresistible if your children are attached to those Finnish books about the Moomintroll family.

Take the escalator down to four, where we'd recommend you march smartly through 15 and 16, passing by two truly terrifying Francis Bacons, and pause in front of Jackson Pollock's spectacular *One, Number 31*. Looking at this, your child is probably thinking, "Wow, I wish they'd let me try that!" Now you're into the land of Rothko and Rauschenberg (look for his *Bed*, with its real, though tiny quilt, pillow, and sheets). In gallery 21, they'll notice what looks like a wrecked car on the wall (John Chamberlain's *Essex*) and from here on you're home free: with the Warhols (*32 Campbell's Soup Cans* and *Marilyn*), Jim Dine's *Five Feet of Colorful Tools* (just what it sounds like), Claes Oldenburg (a giant soft and droopy fan made of black vinyl), and Dan Flavin (neon!). This is about where you will find yourself having a spirited conversation about what constitutes art (and you may end up sounding like your parents).

Having accomplished all this, you can reward yourself and the children with a trip to the third floor (design) for a look at the green Bell helicopter with a bubble cockpit that looks like a dragonfly. See who can be the first to find the sleek E-type Jaguar and, on your way out, you'll all look at the sewing machine, the teakettle, and the Lego pieces with newly open eyes.

- **The Museum of Modern Art**, *11 W. 53rd St., bet. Fifth and Sixth Aves., 212-708-9400, www.moma.org.*
- **Getting there:** *E or V train to Fifth Ave./53rd St.; B, D, or F to 47th-50th St., Rockefeller Ctr.*

Cooler Than Chic: Soho Without (Much) Shopping
Children's Museum of Art...New York Earth Room...cast-iron beauties...Pearl River and Pearl Paint.

Sometimes Soho feels like a large, crowded, over-priced mall. It doesn't have to.

For instance, you can visit the **Children's Museum of Art.** You'll know it by the large zebra standing nonchalantly on the sidewalk outside. What goes on inside this sweet, relaxed, and messy place is hands-on art, a range of activities that work wonderfully for the younger (under seven) set; they can wander in their eccentric way from clay to painting to scrap paper, and at every station there's a friendly person to grab their attention and hold it for as long as the kids are inclined. When they need a change of pace, take them down the stairs for more active delights: a ball pen full of enormous yoga balls (take that, McDonalds!) and a dress-up/theater area where they can strut in creative getups and see themselves on a TV screen overhead. Despite (or perhaps because of) the lack of bells and whistles, this is a place that children genuinely love.

 Take a breather at the **New York Earth Room** on Wooster Street. The entrance is poorly labeled and the stairs are rickety. But once you get to the top you're face-to-face with a permanent installation of crumbly brown earth—280,000 pounds of it—piled to a level height of about twenty-two inches, spread across a white-walled loft space, and separated from you only by a Plexiglas partition that can be reached over. Not much going on here, only the occasional mushroom or weed poking its way up. What's so marvelous is simply the presence of that vast, brown living expanse; it almost seems to breathe. Some people become so attached to it that they come back again and again, and breathe along with it. (Note: the Earth Room is closed from June to September.)

With older children, you can keep walking through Soho, either crisscrossing your way downtown between Broadway and West Broadway or choosing the streets that are our favorites for cast-iron architecture. Greene Street has the most and the best-preserved. Broadway has three real beauties: the Singer Building (1904) at 561–563; the St. Nicholas Hotel at 521–523 (it was used as a Union Army headquarters during the Civil War—look up to see it at its best); and the Haughwout Building at 488–492 (the first building to use a steam safety elevator).

Of course, it wouldn't be a trip to Soho without some shopping, and **Pearl River Mart** has a truly eclectic—even peculiar—range of merchandise at very good prices. We like the Mao hats, mandarin jackets, Chinese dolls, terra cotta soldiers, and the brocade fabric-covered boxes of various sizes, including some in the shape of Chinese take-out food cartons.

For the artsy child, there's no place like **Pearl Paint** on Canal Street. This is the preeminent craft store in the city and not at all kid-centric, so it's good to know what you're looking for before you attack the five floors of beeswax, plaster of Paris, whittling tools, model kits, colored sand, and papier-mâché. When you come out, laden with thrilling purchases, Chinatown (see p. 16) will beckon, but save it for another day.

P.S. The **New York City Fire Museum** is down here and worth a visit for fireman fans, with its impressive displays of vintage equipment, a taxidermied dog from the '30s with a heroic fire-fighting history, and a very loud bell that kids can ring. The excellent gift shop has rubber Dalmatians and fireman transformers, among other treats.

- **Children's Museum of Art**, *182 Lafayette St., bet. Broome and Grand Sts., 212-941- 9198, www.cmany.org.*
- **New York Earth Room**, *141 Wooster St. bet. W. Houston and Prince Sts., 212-473-8072, www.earth-room.org.*
- **Pearl River Mart**, *477 Broadway bet. Broome and Grand Sts., 212-431-4770, www.pearlriver.com.*
- **Pearl Paint**, *308 Canal St., bet. Broadway and Church Sts., 212-431-7932, www.pearlpaint.com.*
- **New York City Fire Museum**, *278 Spring St., bet. Hudson and Varick Sts., 212-691-1303, www.nycfiremuseum.org.*
- **Getting there:** *6 train to Spring St; J, M, N, Q, R, W, Z, or 6 to Canal St; N, R, or W to Prince St.*

The Metropolitan Museum of Art: Civilization x 2
A first foray and a second trip for budding connoisseurs

For that first trip to the Met, stage a quick guerilla raid, and then escape before the sheer size of the place becomes oppressive. Begin with Ancient Egypt: it never fails to enthrall and it's right there on the ground floor, past the recumbent lion. The massive sarcophagi are jaw-dropping, while the 23 Mekutra models (tiny industrious clay people found in a tomb, busily at work carting grain, rowing, and weaving) will bring delighted smiles. William, the Met's blue hippo mascot, is around but not so easy to find; ask a guard for directions. Kids' eyes widen at the sight of the Temple of Dendur, especially when you show them the photos of it *in situ* so that they can grasp the engineering feat that brought it to New York.

Behind the temple, through a glass door, there's a selection from the Burdick Collection of baseball trading cards. These delights will sustain you as you head for the armor. Highlights here include the medieval knights on horseback, a child's suit of armor, and the ferocious samurai warrior in a suit made of steel and leather scales, laced together with leather and silk. Awesome, for once, is the appropriate word. Finally, in complete contrast, decompress in the soothing space of Engelhard Court, an indoor sculpture garden that features a Louis Comfort Tiffany fountain.

For your next visit, go upstairs and find Emanuel Gottlieb Leutze's *Washington Crossing the Delaware*. It is the largest painting in the museum, and the perfect place to start, because of its heroic scale and subject, and also because it contains three glaring historical inaccuracies. If you've read about the painting beforehand in *Inside the Museum* (see below), the kids will have fun finding the mistakes. While you're at it, compare George Washington portraits (the most famous of Gilbert Stuart's is here). Take in the Edward Hoppers and George Caleb Bingham's *Fur Traders Descending the Missouri* en route to the period rooms (building up to a Frank Lloyd Wright living room from a Minnesota house—a low-ceilinged, modernist beauty). Next, walk selectively through the European paintings. Rubens' voluptuous nudes will embarrass most kids, but the perfect details of rustic life in Bruegel's *The Harvesters* or the dotty splendor of the Seurats fascinate. All the big names are here—Rembrandt, Van Gogh, Raphael—but head for surer territory, namely, the Twentieth-Century Wing, which teems with big, bold, witty paintings and structures that grab the attention of young visitors. Next time, they'll have their own favorites to visit.

P.S. The museum does a wonderful book for children called *Inside the Museum* by Joy Richardson. Try to get a copy before you go, and the kids will be primed. Also, the Met's website is an unusually rich resource through which you can view thousands of works from the collections.

- **The Metropolitan Museum of Art**, *1000 Fifth Ave bet. 80th and 84th Sts. 212-535-7710, www.metmuseum.org.*
- **Getting there:** *Take the 4, 5, or 6 train to 86th St. and Lexington Ave.; or B or C to 86th and Central Park West and walk across the park.*

the city's best kept secrets
(right under your nose)

Underground Brooklyn
New York Transit Museum...world's oldest subway tunnel...local food and Trader Joe's...second best city skyline view...Train World for electric trains (don't call them toys)...a glimpse of the City Hall subway stop.

Trains hold enduring fascination for children (not to mention many of their parents) and the **New York Transit Museum** is a wonderful place for both generations to share. It's got enough hands-on exhibits to keep young buffs engaged and enough hardcore history for the serious enthusiast. Start your visit with a quick look through "Steel, Stone, & Backbone," an engaging history of the subway system's construction, punctuated with examples of hundred-year-old equipment—a huge bucket on wheels, lunch pails, and wheelbarrows. There's an outcropping of fake rocks that are excellent for climbing on and video screens showing creaky old black and white movies of laborers heading underground to work. You'll notice the mix of races (this rough, dangerous work was open to immigrants and African-Americans), the lack of helmets or indeed any kind of protective clothing. Occasionally you'll see one of the men wink slyly at the camera. Then on to turnstiles, tokens, and detailed models of the Triborough Bridge and an elevated subway station.

Children will be hard pressed to obey the "Do Not Touch" sign on the wonderful control panel for the Harlem River lift span. Interactive exhibits demonstrate how a soot filter keeps exhaust fumes out of air, how a hybrid diesel-electric engine generates and expends energy and how a fuel cell works. It's not clear how much of this information children can absorb, but they certainly enjoy playing with the exhibits, and they love the mocked-up traffic intersection, with changing lights and two bus driver's seats for "driving," complete with enormous steering wheels and (working) windshield wipers. Skip the exhibit of antique car and train games—in our experience, nothing bores children faster than antique toys—and head down a flight to the track level, where an array of vintage subway cars await, ready to be sat in and strolled through. New Yorkers old enough to remember subway cars with wicker seats, bare light-bulbs and fans whirring away inches above their heads will feel even older. Students of subway strap design will be in heaven, and everyone will get a kick out of the old ads for Burma Shave and war bonds. If you're lucky, you'll meet shy Sadie, the muse-um's resident tabby cat. The gift shop is small but has some treasures, including nicely weighty metal teddy bear key-rings and the Flying Yankee windup tin train, with its three very shiny cars for $9.95. There's plenty of Thomas the Tank Engine stuff and the Brio-minded will be pleased to find compatible track that is much less expensive than Brio's.

Another subway attraction is just a couple of blocks away; it's **Brooklyn's subway tunnel, which is also the world's old-est**. This is the singular passion of its (re)discoverer, Brooklyn native and railroad buff Robert Diamond who, as a student at Brooklyn College, spent months poring over ancient docu-ments and newspapers and annoying city officials with his investigations. When Diamond finally got permission to poke around underground, he went down a manhole at the intersec-tion of Atlantic and Court Streets, broke through a wall, and felt a 150-year-old breeze blowing into his face.

That was in 1979. Since then, Mr. Diamond and some hard-core volunteers, the Brooklyn Historic Railway Association, have been slowly excavating the site. About a quarter of a mile of tunnel has been cleared. Mr. Diamond wants to keep digging right through to the waterfront in Red Hook, where the track begins. He has more plans too, which he will enthusiastically share with you when he's not explaining tunnel-boring technol-ogy of the 1840s and why the developer who built the tunnel had it sealed less than twenty-five years later. Diamond's a spellbinding raconteur, and he has a few bloodcurdling anec-dotes that will delight the children. (For instance, one unpopu-lar foreman was murdered and mixed into the mortar, so he is still, literally, on-site.) The tunnel entrance down that manhole is a squeeze, and folks with claustrophobic leanings will feel a frisson. But the brick-lined tunnel itself, with its impressively high, arched ceiling, is stately and calming. The silence is total, with no hint of the traffic thundering above. Bring a flashlight and comfy shoes, and keep your eyes peeled for crickets, old nails and hardware, and nineteenth-century graffiti.

Back on Atlantic, the first thing you'll see is the spanking new branch of **Trader Joe's** (or, if it's delayed, the site of the spanking new Trader Joe's). Let's hear it for gourmet snacks! The true local hero is a little way west on Atlantic: **Sahadi**, the Middle Eastern Zabar's, in business since 1898. Here you can buy Swiss chocolate bars, loose spices, fresh halvah, olives of every conceivable type, dried fruit, pistachios by the bushel, great hummus, and keftah for supper at home—aaah! The aromas are great, and so are the prices. No credit cards, though.

You can't leave the neighborhood without investing in some sweet, sticky Middle Eastern pastries and cookies—stock up on them and on spinach pies at the **Damascus Bread & Pastry Shop**, a few doors down from Sahadi.

On this or another trip, walk a few blocks through the leafy, narrow streets of Brooklyn Heights to the Promenade, and enjoy the extraordinary view of Manhattan (remembering, of course, that the true connoisseur favors the view from under the Brooklyn Bridge, see page 89). If the Promenade looks familiar even though you've never been there before, it's because every advertising spread in New York City seems to be shot there.

There's one more essential stop in Brooklyn for the train-obsessed. That's **Train World**, the biggest train shop in New York City (also the place where Bobby Bacala of *The Sopranos* got whacked). Many of the customers are adult hobbyists, men intent on enhancing their setups, and there is much banter between them and the staff about sneaking new purchases past the wife. Kids just starting with model trains will find this cluttered place irresistible. It stocks everything from diminutive N-scale trains to the mighty G type. You can spend thousands on collectibles, but simple starter sets (a circle of track, an engine, a few cars) can be had for $50 or so. And for less than that, you can acquire the tackle that's crucial to the model railroader: smoke-producing fluid, extra track, tiny people, and trees.

P.S. Here's how train aficionados in your home can steal a glimpse of the ornate and unused **City Hall subway station**, which is rented out to television and film producers: Take the East Side downtown local to the last stop. Remain in the last car while it turns around for the uptown journey. You can see the station from the back window as the train pivots by.

- **New York Transit Museum**, *at the corner of Boerum Pl. and Schermerhorn St., Brooklyn, 718-694-1600, www.mta.info/mta/museum.*
- **Subway Tunnel**, *tours begin outside the Independence Savings Bank (to be Trader Joe's) on the southwest corner of Court St. and Atlantic Ave. Call the Historic Brooklyn Railroad Association for dates and times, 718-941-3160, www.brooklynrail.net.*
- **Trader Joe's**, *Independence Savings Bank, southwest corner of Atlantic and Court Sts., opening 2008, www.traderjoes.com.*
- **Sahadi Importing Co. Inc.**, *187 Atlantic Ave., bet. Clinton and Court Sts., 718-624-4550, www.sahadis.com.*
- **Damascus Bread & Pastry Shop Ltd.**, *195 Atlantic Ave., bet. Clinton and Court Sts., 718-625-7070.*
- **Getting there:** *Transit Museum and Subway Tunnel: 2, 3, and 4 trains to Borough Hall; M or R to Court Street, A, C, or F to Jay St./Borough Hall.*
- **Train World**, *751 McDonald Ave. at Ditmas Ave., 718-436-707, www.trainworld.com.*
- **Getting there:** *F train to Ditmas Ave.*

In the Shadow of the Great Gray Bridge
Fort Washington Park and the Little Red Lighthouse...The Cloisters.

Unless you live in the neighborhood, just getting to **Fort Washington Park** is a challenge. But it's worth it. This little-known strip of green runs along the west shore of Manhattan, parallel to Washington Heights and right next to the water, from 155th Street to Dyckman Street. It offers great views of the river and the Palisades, woodsy trails, loads of facilities—baseball diamonds, basketball, and tennis courts, a playground—and an ambience that's dreamy and tucked-away.   During spring and summer the baseball diamonds are always in use, mostly by Little League teams, but (take note, tennis players) the courts are seldom fully occupied.

And of course it's got the **Little Red Lighthouse**.

Since it's not easily seen from our shores (or even the George Washington Bridge), the lighthouse has assumed mythic status as something everybody's heard of but no one's visited. But there it is, tiny and red and nestled sweetly at water's edge right under the GWB—just as it is in Hildegarde Hoyt Swift's classic story, *The Little Red Lighthouse and the Great Gray Bridge:*

> It was round and fat and red.
> It was fat and red and jolly.
> And it was VERY, VERY PROUD.

The 85-and-counting-year-old lighthouse sits on rocks where there once stood a gibbet used to execute pirates. During spring and summer, it's occasionally open for the Urban Park Rangers' free walking tours, so call for the schedule.

Inside, the building is a small, empty cylinder, with a spiral staircase snaking up to the observation deck. A tiny parapet runs around the outside and you can walk on it, making sure to hold small hands firmly—the breezes are brisker than you'd expect. Safely down, read the nearby plaque which celebrates the efforts of children all over the country to save the lighthouse when, in 1951, the Coast Guard planned to demolish it; apparently, the children's distress managed to soften even the stony heart of Robert Moses, who was Parks Commissioner at the time.

Be warned. There are no amenities here—no food concessions, no public bathrooms. But if you come up in September for the Little Red Lighthouse Festival, you'll find a very jolly scene. There's a stage set up for bluegrass singers, storytellers, and sea-shanty types; Rangers stand good-naturedly around venerable boats once used on the Hudson; and earnest people at folding tables will hand you literature about ways to insure the future well-being of the Hudson. The kids will love the low-tech games (Noc-Hockey and Ping-Pong), the horse-drawn-wagon rides, face-painting, barbecued hamburgers and locally caught bluefish—grilled and presented on toothpicks. Why not bring a picnic? There's usually an excellent T-shirt featuring the lighthouse for sale. Once home again, you'll feel you spent the afternoon at a village fair.

Having come this far, treat yourself to **The Cloisters**, which is in Fort Tryon Park, about fifteen blocks to the north. (And if you haven't eaten, consider the **New Leaf Café**, a welcome new addition to the park. But before you go, look at the menu online—the choices might be a little sophisticated for young palates.)

Once at The Cloisters, your number one destination is the Unicorn Tapestries. The drama and the mystery of this woven narrative crosses generations effortlessly. The knights' sarcophagi will prove to the children that there really were such people as knights. In the Treasury, seek out the illuminated manuscripts, and the sixteenth-century rosary bead carved from boxwood. The size of a walnut, it opens like a locket and has unfolding panels that form a triptych depicting scenes from the life of Christ. The detail is incredible. Literally hundreds of minute figures are carved into this bead, complete with facial expressions, fingernails, and hair.

Next, stroll around the enclosed gardens, the cloisters themselves. The bare stone rooms and gloomy staircases right off the gardens are perfect for a quick round of fantasy play, because no matter how earnestly you explain what a cloistered monastery was, your kids will feel that this is a castle and act accordingly. So be prepared to stand on the parapet and look at the brilliant view—you might think you're in a castle too.

- **Little Red Lighthouse:** *Fort Washington Park at 181st St. (Call Urban Park Rangers at 311 to find out when the lighthouse is open and the day of the festival.) www.nyc-*

govparks.org.

- **Getting there:** *Take the A train to 181st St. and walk west until you see the uptown leg of the Drive and a footbridge crossing it. Take the bridge and continue bearing left, downhill, toward the base of the George Washington Bridge.*
- **The Cloisters**, *Fort Tryon Park, 212-923-3700, www.met-museum.org/collections/department.asp?dep=7*
- **New Leaf Café**, *One Margaret Corbin Dr., Fort Tryon Park, 212-568-5323, www.nyrp.org/newleaf.*
- **Getting there:** *Take the A train to 190th St. Leave the station via the elevator and walk up through Fort Tryon Park.*

  P.S. If you've got the time and the temperament, substitute a leisurely bus ride for the subway home. The M4 bus goes from The Cloisters all the way down upper Broadway, crossing east on 110th St. and continuing down Fifth Ave. Stare out the windows at the absorbing, changing cityscape before you.

Three Cheers for Pooh! For Who? For Pooh!
The real Pooh and friends...Sony Wonder Technology Lab...a picnic in the plaza.

Winnie-the-Pooh.

The very name retains its hold over even the most determinedly current child. Take yours upstairs at the **Donnell Library** on 53rd Street to see the actual, original Winnie-the-Pooh toys that once belonged to A. A. Milne's son Christopher (a.k.a. Christopher Robin), and inspired the illustrator E. H. Shepard. More than seventy years old, dilapidated, and loved-to-death, the original Eeyore, Tigger, Piglet, Kanga, and, of course, the divine Pooh, still have soul. You'd recognize them anywhere; you'll want to take them home. People around the world have somehow learned that these animals are in New York. They make pilgrimages to see them and write heartfelt messages in the visitors' book. Remember to buy a postcard before you leave!

For something completely d[...]
you could move on to the **Sony** [...]
Sony Plaza on Madison Avenue, w[...]
and up can mess around on the c[...]
tions by working some very fanc[...]
exhibit, located in Sony Plaza, is s[...] [...], courtly
guys direct you to a glass elevator that zooms up four floors
from the atrium and deposits you at the lab. Next, you have to
log in, which you do by recording your name, image, and voice.
A little key card is issued you, which is then used to access the
machines. All this procedure is deeply impressive to the kids,
and before you've even really started!

As for the machines, you can play recording engineer as
you tinker with the mix for a music tape. See how medical
imaging works—press many buttons to help solve an environmental crisis (oil spill, approaching hurricane), work robots, play
video games, use sound and light special effects, and so on.

It's all very clear and orderly—you just pick your machine,
sit down, and log in. At the end, you get a graduation certifi-
cate with your name, picture, and list of accomplishments on it.
Regular admittance to this excellent place is first-come, first-
serve, so there's often a line. Book in advance or try to come
when it's not teeming with school groups—they take prece-
dence in the mornings.

Afterwards, sit with a snack in the light-filled, bustling atrium. There's a café with pastries and, inevitably, a Starbucks in
the Sony Style store. If you've planned ahead (some people are
that well-organized!), you could settle everybody down with a
picnic from home and finish with ice-cream.

Whatever you choose, you'll find this a pleasant place for
serious people-watching. If everyone's truly starving, just
around the corner on Madison you'll find a branch of trusty
Burger Heaven, the old-school New York chain that serves
excellent sandwiches, salads, chili, and many kinds of (very
good) burgers.

Note: The Donnell Library is scheduled for demolition in
fall 2008, at which time Pooh and the gang will move to the

...nch. The good news is that they're staying in town.
...onnell Library Center (Children's Room), 20 W. 53rd
St., bet. 5th and 6th Aves., 212-621-0636,
www.nypl.org/branch/central/dlc/dch.

- **Sony Wonder Technology Lab**, *Sony Plaza, 550 Madison Ave., bet. 55th and 56th Sts., 212-833-8100, www.sonywondertechlab.com.*
- **Burger Heaven**, *536 Madison Ave., bet. 54th and 55th Sts., 212-753-4214, www.burgerheaven.com.*
- **Getting there:** *4, 5, 6, N or R trains to 59th St.; E and V to Fifth Ave.; F to 57th St.*

And Staten Island Zoo (1)

*Snug Harbor Cultural Center...Children's Museum...
Botanical Gardens...Staten Island Zoo...Alice Austen
House...supper overlooking the Kill Van Kull.*

The truth is that much of Staten Island is a best-kept secret (except to Staten Islanders). Riding the Staten Island Ferry is always a delight. But Staten Island's public transportation on the weekends can be sleepy and infrequent, which is not so good for an excursion with or without the kids. So visit by car or bring something for the children to play with while you wait for your bus or train.

If you drive, you'll feel that you've left the city as you cruise along quiet streets with frame houses, tidy lawns, and masses of utility wires overhead. Focus your trip around either the **Snug Harbor Cultural Center** or the zoo. You could manage to see both in one day, but you'd miss out on the small-town feeling of the island and the many charms of these attractions.

The Snug Harbor estate was built in the 1830s by a reformed and retired pirate—well, privateer—as a safe haven for retired mariners. He chose a site on a hill overlooking the waters of the Kill Van Kull, with a sweeping view of Manhattan. The buildings are a glorious mix of grand, cream-colored, colonnaded Greek Revivals that once contained dormitories, dining and meeting halls, and fairy tale-like dormered cottages where the staff lived. The Snug Harbor complex houses museums and performance spaces, which occasionally have events for children.

For your first trip, though, you should focus on the **Children's Museum**, a cheerful hands-on place with several distinct areas for playing and learning: outsize board games, a bug exhibit (with an ant hill kids can crawl into and exoskeletons they can try on), a room full of big blocks, a little stage with an array of costumes and props, an outdoor area with nautical features like boats, a crow's nest, and a little lighthouse. Large, inviting-looking sculptures dot the lawns and loom under the trees; the giant wooden grasshopper is excellent for climbing. There are also some artists' installations on hand, each designed to have small persons walk through, touch, or peer into them. Even the smallest kids will be comfortable here, sloshing around in the water play area while their older siblings exclaim over the live, dead, and outsize grubs upstairs.

Most of Snug Harbor's grounds are open to the public: 80 acres, with lawns, a duck pond, and the Botanical Gardens. Treat yourself to a walk through the famous **Chinese Scholar's Garden**, with its serene courtyards and walkways, its streams and bamboo. If you're lucky, the children will be intrigued enough to let you take in some of its contemplative beauty. When they begin to fade, take them to the **Lion's Sensory Garden**, which is designed to appeal to the senses of smell, hearing, and touch as well as sight. Weather permitting, the gardens and grounds are great for picnicking. Melville's Café in the Visitors' Center has simple tasty fare.

A little way inland from Snug Harbor, the **Staten Island Zoo** feels like a well-planned, small-town zoo. Ride a pony, check out the porcupines, and feed the cows and ducks while hoping that the restless goats will stage a breakout (it happens). The surprising highlight is the reptile house. It's large, dim, and very well-stocked with turtles, snakes both vast and tiny, sharks and rays, iguanas and lizards. It's all on a scale that children are happy with—no lines, no jostling, but still impressive. You can buy adequate snacks to eat at outside tables, and the gift shop is small and inviting.

While you're on the Island, don't miss another of its amazing views—this time, from the **Alice Austen House**, right on the water on Hylan Boulevard, across the street from a hideous high-rise. Originally a simple farmhouse, it was remodeled into a pastoral fantasy cottage by Alice Austen, the Victorian photographer who inherited it. The low-ceilinged downstairs rooms are shady and intimate, and on the walls are Austen's pictures of her family and friends at picnics and tennis parties, as well as haunting shots of the view, which has certainly changed over the course of a hundred years, as you will see when you step outside onto the lawns. They slope down gently to a rocky beach, littered with city debris that will prove fascinating to the younger members. Relax—you're more likely to find worn bottle glass, driftwood, and pieces of old foam or tubing than the dreaded medical waste. Up and down, right in front of you, pass the ships and tankers. To your immediate right (you certainly can't miss it) is the lofty sweep of the Verrazano-Narrows Bridge. Directly across is Brooklyn, and to your left, that inescapable Manhattan skyline. It's rare to find such a huge view in the city, rarer still to find it from the private grounds of a little white house with filigree decoration and a long Dutch roof.

There's plenty of fast food around, but we suggest you take Bay Street and then Richmond Terrace around the tip of the island, a little way past Snug Harbor. On the right, by the water, you will find **R. H. Tugs**. Although it has enough wood paneling and unfamiliar items on the menu (jambalaya? mesclun?) to prompt subdued behavior in the youngest, Tugs will be more than happy to provide anybody who so desires with plain pasta, a burger, a BLT, or a big plate of french fries. The adult food is just fine. Meanwhile, the power stations and moorings of scenic Bayonne are on view just outside the big windows, as is the occasional monolithic container ship on its way up the Kill. As you eat, you can sense the workings of a still-busy harbor.

- **Snug Harbor Cultural Center and Gardens**, *1000 Richmond Terr., Staten Island, 718-448-2500, www.snug-harbor.org.*
- **Staten Island Children's Museum**, *at Snug Harbor, 718-273-2060, www.statenislandkids.org.*

- **Staten Island Zoo**, *614 Broadway, 718-442-3101 or 3100 (tape), www.statenislandzoo.org.*
- **Alice Austen House**, *2 Hylan Blvd. at Edgewater St., 718-816-4506, www.aliceausten.org.*
- **R. H. Tugs**, *1115 Richmond Terr., 718-447-6369, www.rhtugs.com.*
- **Getting there:**
  For the Staten Island Ferry Terminal, take the 1, 9, N, or R train to South Ferry and follow the signs (call 718-815-BOAT for schedules).

  By bus from the Ferry in Staten Island: For Snug Harbor, the S40 from the Staten Island Ferry; for the zoo, the S48 to Broadway, then walk three blocks; for the Alice Austen House, the S51 to Bay St./Hylan Blvd.; for R. H. Tugs, the S40, a few blocks from Snug Harbor.

  By car: Verrazano-Narrows Bridge to Staten Island Expressway. Call or consult websites for more specific directions.

And Staten Island Too (2)
Fort Wadsworth

The forts at either end of the soaring Verrazzano Narrows Bridge are among the oldest military installations in the country, the guardians of New York Harbor for more than 150 years. Fort Hamilton, on the Brooklyn side, is still an active army base, as well as home to the Harbor Defense Museum (see p. 37). On the Staten Island side, **Fort Wadsworth** has been a part of the Gateway National Recreation area since 1995. It's a wonderful place to visit, a perfect mix of crumbly, atmospheric ruin and imposing stone fortification, with grassy hillsides where everyone can decompress while inhaling stiff sea breezes.

For years, the fort was allowed to deteriorate and many of its old structures were abandoned. Today, much of the 226-acre site is open to visitors. You and yours can take the self-guided tour at your own pace, checking out abandoned gun batteries half-hidden in the undergrowth. Be sure to pause at the Overlook for the spectacular view of the Upper and Lower New

York Bays. But to see things off-limits to the casual explorer, join one of the guided tours that start from the Visitor's Center, three blocks inside the Bay Street Gate on the left. There's a twelve-minute film shown here, recommended for ages eight and up, that makes a good preface to the tour.

The oldest building is the massive Battery Weed, begun in 1847. Built right at the water's edge, it's a looming stone structure with three levels of cannon-ports (space for 116 big guns) and great echoes. The guide will explain how cannons worked in a way that you can all understand, and will lead you off to see the nineteenth-century latrine and make ghoulish jokes for the kids. Legend has it that there are hidden tunnels and passageways between the gun emplacements.

On top of the hill sits Fort Tompkins, the barracks, where about 600 soldiers were housed. Here, you'll thread your way through so many identical, cool, vaulted-brick passageways that you'll feel as if you're in a maze. This impregnable-seeming place has two sets of walls (the granite outer walls are four feet thick and more than thirty high) with a space in between where attackers could be trapped in a crossfire; the guide will point out that the rifle slits in each wall are "offset"—that is, not placed directly opposite each other to minimize the risk of shooting a comrade by accident. On our first trip, our guide encouraged us to linger in the pitch-black powder magazine, where gunpowder was stored in utter darkness, the better to protect it from sparks. The room, he informed the rapt children in our group, contained a ghost named George. Fortunately, George was shy that day.

Save some time after the tour for exploring; you'll find great surprises along the trails; an observation post with a rusty phone installation from which the officers could track cannon fire and phone in course corrections; the burned-out railhead where mines were unloaded. The lighthouse is open to the public and there's a handsome row of officers' houses. If you go in the spring, wildflowers will be blooming in the woods. Bring a picnic.

- **Fort Wadsworth, Gateway National Recreation Area,** *south end of Bay Street, Staten Island, 718-354-4500,* *www.nps.gov/gate.*

- **Getting there:** *By car, cross the Verrazzano-Narrows Bridge, lower level, take Bay St. exit, turn right and keep going. Or take the Staten Island Ferry and, at the St. George Terminal, the S51 bus.*

Terminal Delights
Grand Central Station...Whispering Gallery...tours... sky-bridge...shopping and food court favorites.

New York's magnificent railroad portal (official name: **Grand Central Terminal**) is a destination in itself, full of sights, shops and great food. The mighty Main Concourse, all creamy marble and sweeping staircases, is familiar. But look up at the beloved sea-blue zodiac ceiling and note that the constellations are, in fact, backwards. Why? Apparently, the painter took his cue from a medieval manuscript that showed the heavens as seen from outside the celestial sphere. See if the kids can find the tiny square of darker blue that marks the color the ceiling used to be before the renovation.

Downstairs is the secret **Whispering Gallery**, just outside the entrance to the Oyster Bar & Restaurant, the station's oldest business. Here, three beautifully tiled and vaulted corridors meet. Stand at the corners of the intersection, diagonally across from each other, and take turns speaking softly and directly into the wall. The person across the way will hear every word you say. Amazing! You can experience the same effect in the Oyster Bar, too, which is why you can hear people across the dining room more clearly than those sitting next to you. (You probably don't want to test this out with the children in the restaurant.)

The Municipal Arts Society has a free weekly tour of the station every Wednesday at 12:30. It's not designed for young children, but your pre-teen or teenager with a special interest in architecture or the history of New York, would love it. Colorful facts abound. Did you know that if you were to roll a ball down from the main entrance, it wouldn't stop until it reached the trains? Or that the clock on the 42nd Street façade contains the world's largest example of Tiffany glass? The high-light of the tour is a walk across one of the "skybridges," narrow passages inside the high windows that dominate the building's sides. The public is not permitted in here; the scurrying figures in the concourse below don't even notice you four floors above them, walking between walls of glass. It's an unforgettable experience.

The station is always staging special events—one spring they had both "Meet Mickey Dolenz" and Tartan Week. Around the holidays, there's a very appealing gift fair and a "kaleidoscope light show" playing out across the ceiling as festive music plays.

Don't forget the regular shops. The Transit Museum's Gallery and Shop has great souvenirs (the same as in the shop at the New York Transit Museum, see p. 50) and, for you, at least one book you can't live without, *Subway Cars of the BMT*. In the Lexington Passage, you'll find the Kids' General Store (sock monkeys, Mayan blocks, origami) and, down one level, the Dining Concourse, with its dizzying array of excellent fast-food choices: Jamaican patties, Two Boots pizza, Eat-a-Pita, Chinese, Japanese, Mexican, you name it. For dessert, there's the Little Pie Company or cheesecake from Junior's.

- **Grand Central Terminal**, *E. 42nd St. at Park Ave., 212-532-4900, www.grandcentralterminal.com.*
- **Municipal Arts Society**, *212-935-3960, www.mas.org.*
- **Getting there:** *the 4, 5, 6, 7, or S train to Grand Central.*

B.P.C.P.F.s
Stands for Battery Park City Park Favorites

Battery Park City is confusing if you don't live there. It's so tranquil, so sleek, so unlike the rest of New York. Its waterside parks teem with wonderful attractions for small children, so it's worth exploring. We've picked out two especially lovely places for kids to play.

Nelson Rockefeller Park: Way west on Chambers Street,

you come to the gently curving staircases that take you down to it. Immediately on your left is a secluded, walled area which is the home of "The Real World," a much-loved sculptural exhibit by Tom Otterness. There's a meandering path with big pennies embedded in it, and all around tiny bronze people and animals—and a few large ones—perch on benches, follow each other down the path, or lie down for a rest. There's a little pool framed with piles of pennies (pennies again—this is the Financial District, after all) and more eccentric people and animals. If your kids love this, which they will, you can take them to see more Otterness in the equally inspired but rather less salubrious setting of a subway station (p. 120). Walk south and you'll see soft lawns and benches and a spiffy, state-of-the-art playground with chain-link climbing nets, animal-head fountains, and a foot-powered red carousel. Heaven.

Further on is the Play House, where smiley park personnel hand out board games, jump ropes, ping-pong paddles, and information. You can play Noc-Hockey, or roll around with the big puffy lawn toys. There are swings for older kids and handball and basketball courts. (For those who care, and we do, Steve Nash of the Phoenix Suns has been known to join in pickup games there.) And there's always the river alongside and people running, biking, and roller-blading by. It's a slice of the city at play. To end your trip, why not have lunch outside from one of the restaurants in North Cove, just in front of the World Financial Center's Winter Garden? Watch the yachts bobbing at anchor and look out across the bustle of the river to the Colgate sign.

P.S. There are some (very discreetly indicated) toilets around. You'll see their location on the maps on the dark green signposts. The Winter Garden has public toilets too, but you may need radar to find them.

Teardrop Park: This secluded jewel is just inland from Rockefeller Park, with apartment buildings looming all around it. Its two hilly, rocky acres offer unstructured play of the best kind. The pathways are lined with native plants; there's a pond, spacious sand pits, and well-tended lawns for relaxing in the sun, but the crowd-pleasers are a slide and a wall. The slide is steep (set into a rocky slope), metal, and twenty-eight feet long. Kids clamber up the rocks to reach the top of the slide, fill a bucket from the convenient fountain, then hurl the water down the slide, then the bucket, then themselves. Don't worry, it's less death-defying than it sounds. As for the wall, it's 300 tons of craggy Hudson Valley bluestone. In winter, recycled water from the eco-luxe Solaire apartment building is directed to flow over it, forming a spectacular ice wall. Coming soon (maybe they've secretly arrived already): twenty salamanders as permanent residents. Look for them!

- **Nelson A. Rockefeller Park**, *north end of Battery Park City, from Chambers St. all the way down to the World Financial Center.*
- **Teardrop Park**, *between Warren and Murray Sts., North End Ave. and River Terrace.*
  You'll find a mass of information about all the Battery Park City Parks Conservancy goings-on at www.bpc-parks.org.
  - **Getting there:** *Take the A, C, J, M, Z, 1, 2, 3, 4, 5, 9, E, or R to Fulton St./Broadway-Nassau.*

fabulous festivities:
unusual celebrations and fresh takes on the old reliables

Independence Night in Williamsburg or Greenpoint

Bored on the 4th of July? If you're not lucky enough to have a convenient rooftop from which to watch the Macy's July 4th fireworks display, we suggest Williamsburg, the artsy waterfront enclave that is gentrifying at an astounding rate.

Once upon a time, Williamsburg was populated almost exclusively by immigrants—and this cosmopolitan neighborhood is still home to Hasidic Jews, Poles, Puerto Ricans, Dominicans, and Italians—but now, the place teems with restaurants, clubs, and galleries. Luxury apartment buildings are going up along the shore and the homesteading artists of twenty years ago must be forgiven for muttering, "There goes the neighborhood."

Still, nobody's complaining about the new **East River State Park**, situated right on the water on the two-block-long site of the Brooklyn Eastern District Terminal. This small gem has native plantings and "historic Terminal remnants" (that means trackbeds). Most importantly, it's right across from the fireworks barge. It will surely be jam-packed on the 4th, but less so than the FDR Drive.

Aficionados of post-industrial decay will be delighted by the faded sign denoting the former Ko-Rec Type factory across Kent Avenue on the corner of North 10th Street on Bedford and Berry. Just a few blocks inland, there are many places to eat, but we favor the artfully funky and (be warned) extremely popular **Pies 'n' Thighs**, a few blocks south on Kent.

If the park seems too crowded or too much of a scene, go a few blocks further north to one of the **Greenpoint piers** off India Street or Huron, where you'll encounter a benign and festive mix of Eastern Europeans and more recently arrived young people from Manhattan. The only problem is that unless you're driving, you'll have to summon up your resolve and take the G train. You've heard of it, haven't you?

- **East River State Park**, *Kent Ave. bet. N. 7th and 9th Sts., Brooklyn.*

- **Getting there:** *L to Bedford Ave., walk east down N. 7th to Kent Ave.*
- **Pies 'n' Thighs**, *351 Kent Ave. at S. 5th St., Brooklyn, 347-282-6005, www.piesandthighs.com.*
- **India St. and Huron St. piers**, *off West St., Brooklyn.*
- **Getting there:** *E or F to Queens Plaza or L to Metropolitan Ave. then transfer to the G, getting off at Greenpoint Ave. Walk east on Greenpoint Ave. to West St. Turn right and go three blocks to India St., four to Huron. The piers are on your left.*

Old Home Day at Historic Richmond Town

This autumn extravaganza is held on the third Sunday in October at Staten Island's Historic Richmond Town, which is New York City's answer to Williamsburg, Virginia. The village, a couple of dozen houses in various stages of restoration spread over what was once the provincial heart of Staten Island, is worth a visit at any time, but it's particularly jolly at this time of year. All the buildings are open, and friendly locals clad in period dress stroll the village streets, sit in front parlors, and demonstrate traditional crafts and trades like candle-making and chair caning. The blacksmith, laboring with hammer, tongs and roaring forge, draws oohs and aahs. We once saw a gent in buckskins demonstrate the action on a muzzle-loading rifle he seemed to have built by himself, or at least been heavily involved with.

All the guides and demonstrators really know their stuff and play their parts with gravity and poise, but when the kids need to blow off some steam, find the hay jump, and let them hurl themselves over and over again from an enormous mound of hay onto a smaller mound of hay. It looks so therapeutic, you'll wish you had this at work.

You can buy hearth-prepared soup, bread, and cider at the tavern, right near the roof-raising demo. If the Home Brewers of Staten Island are on hand, you can buy some authentic root beer but not, alas, their more serious beverages. They'll give you a little cup of beer, porter, or stout for free, though. A shuttle bus runs regularly to nearby Decker Farm, which is the only functioning farm left in New York City. There, you can pick a pumpkin (every Saturday and Sunday in October). Check the website for details.

As the light starts to fade, mosey down to the gristmill and watch it actually mill grist, then see if there are any ducks left on the pond behind. You're in New York City. Isn't that weird? If you haven't filled up on Colonial soup, there are plenty of lively restaurants on Hylan Boulevard, the long commercial strip you'll travel to get home by car.

- **Historic Richmond Town**, *441 Clarke Ave., Staten Island, 718-351-1611, www.historicrichmondtown.org.*
- **Getting there:** *From the Staten Island Ferry: Take the S74 bus from the terminal to Richmond Road and St. Patrick's Place.*

Powwows

Three or four times a year, representatives from Native American tribes all around the country (as well as from Central and South America) gather in the metropolitan area—at parks or other big outdoor venues—to compete in dancing, chanting, and drumming, to sell their craftwork, and raise public consciousness of their tribal identities.

Powwows are great fun to visit, especially when the dancing starts. The drummers, who sit huddled together, establish a groove and the chanters begin their hypnotic drone. Gradually men, women, and children begin to circle, shuffle, and leap. The drummers begin to improvise, taking their cues from each other. The sound and the swirling feathers and buckskin are thrilling; children realize immediately that this is the real thing.

Don't miss the crafts, such as beaded belts, real (toy) spears, and bows and arrows made of wood by real tribespeople. And try the food—everything from excellent buffalo burgers, chili, and Indian tacos to fried bread sprinkled with powdered sugar.

Powwows of various sizes go on at various locations in the city and environs, including New Jersey and Connecticut. The largest and most impressive is the **Gateway to the Nations**, which is sometimes held at Floyd Bennett Field in Brooklyn. For dates and locations, watch the newspaper, call the Red Hawk Indian Arts Council (718-686-9297) or visit its website at www.redhawkcouncil.org.

P.S. Kids with an interest in Native American culture will enjoy the **National Museum of the American Indian** in the spectacular Customs House building at the Battery. The museum's mission is to convey the experience of being an Indian rather than relating an objectified history of battles and tribes. This means an emphasis on domestic and ceremonial objects with commentary by living Indians, which is fascinating. For younger children, there are plenty of simple, interactive exhibits, such as drawers to open which contain artifacts that can be handled: Pan pipes, toy lacrosse sticks, woven fabrics. There is no permanent collection here, so exhibits change regularly. On our visits, the objects on display have included breathtaking animal masks, 1,800-year-old duck decoys, jewelry made of beads, quills, and feathers. Before you leave, stop to look at the lavish Reginald Marsh ceiling murals in the rotunda, and visit the gift shop for lovely, reasonably-priced souvenirs—trouble dolls, arrowheads, ocarinas, and hackysacks.

- **National Museum of the American Indian**, *1 Bowling Green, 212-514-3700, www.nmai.si.edu.*
- **Getting there:** *4 or 5 to Bowling Green; 1 to South Ferry; R or W to Whitehall St.; M, J, or Z to Broad St.; Bus: M1, M6, or M15 to South Ferry.*

Tugboat Race

Stuck in town over Labor Day weekend? That's great, because you get to watch the **Annual Tugboat Race & Competition**. For fifteen years and counting, the Working Harbor Committee has sponsored this wonderful event, which brings throngs of people to the West Side waterfront to see and cheer the only boats deserving of the term "adorable." They're a lot more than cute, however, and on this day they show off what they can do.

Things kick off with the tugboat parade, which starts around 10 a.m. on the Sunday of Labor Day weekend. The boats, of all sizes and vintages, gather near Pier 84, at 44th Street and Twelfth Avenue, before setting off for the starting line uptown by the 79th Street Boat Basin. They're accompanied by fireboats spraying great arcs of water overhead and sometimes by a fearsome-looking Coast Guard cutter. The race, one nautical mile in length, starts at 11 and is thrilling. A dozen or more tugs tearing full-throttle down the river is a remarkable sight to behold, and quite something to listen to as well. There's only one winner, of course, but awards are given in several different horsepower categories.

After the race, there are more contests to show off the tugboats' strength and their crews' skill; they take place off Pier 84. In the "nose-to-nose" pushing contest, pairs of tugs face off bow-to-bow and attempt to push each other backwards. The line toss, in which tugs approach the pier and are timed as a crew member attempts to "lasso" a bollard without the boat touching the pier, requires tremendous coordination between captain and line handler.

Finally, there's the awards ceremony on the pier: In addition to prizes given to the race and other contest winners, there are awards for best-dressed crew, best-looking tug, best tugboat mascot, best historic tug and best crew member tattoo (that can legally be displayed). It's all over by 3 and then you can go home and reread *Scuffy the Tugboat* with renewed vigor.

- **Annual Tugboat Race & Competition**, *starting at Pier 84, W. 44th St. and Hudson River, 212-757-1600, (Working Harbor Committee), www.workingharbor.com.*
- **Getting there:** *A, C, E, or 7 to 42nd St/ Port Authority. Walk west to 12th Ave. and north two blocks. By bus, take M42 west to the Circle Line Pier.*

Tibetan Festival

The Jacques Marchais Museum of Tibetan Art is a calm, secluded place, built to resemble a Himalayan mountain temple. It sits on the side of a steep hill, overlooking terraced gardens and a lily pond with fish in it. On a clear day, there's a distant view of Lower New York Bay. This little gem is open from April to November and we highly recommend it for anyone who's willing to go to Staten Island for an island of tranquility.

But the time to take your kids is in October, for the **Tibetan Festival.** The mood is serene as ever, but there's also plenty for the kids to do and see. They can cut out and color paper mandalas or yaks. There's a prayer flag-raising ceremony and an ancient-seeming, artful puppet show that, unbelievably enough, you may actually enjoy watching with your children. Artisans and dealers sell Tibetan art (some quite gorgeous and expensive) and wares in the garden, and your kids will enjoy some of the Tibetan food buffet (truly—the bread is soft and flat, like pita, and the vegetable dumplings are mild and savory).

The one-room museum is dimly lit and atmospheric. It holds a three-tiered altar with gleaming figures in gold, silver, and bronze; many intricate carvings, a ceremonial apron made entirely of human bone; and a chart called the "Histomap of Religion: The Story of Man's Search for Spiritual Unity." Children will be impressed, most of all, with the monks—rapt men in saffron robes who chant and ring little bells for hours on end. There are usually four or five of them present, and the spell they cast is palpable. Whether you're a believer or not, a child or an adult, the sound is balm for the soul. The museum is about four miles past Richmond Town.

- **Jacques Marchais Museum of Tibetan Art**, *338 Lighthouse Ave., Staten Island, 718-987-3500, www.tibetanmuseum.org.*
- **Getting there:** *S74 bus from the Staten Island Ferry Terminal.*

The Christmas Lights of Dyker Heights

This comfortable, largely Italian neighborhood overlooks the Verrazano-Narrows Bridge and Gravesend Bay. Many of its homes are palaces, representing a wide range of architectural traditions from antebellum Southern to Tudor to ranch.

During the holiday season, houses here both large and small are tricked out in the most extravagant Christmas decorations seen outside of Rockefeller Center. Yards teem with light-encrusted trees, Nativity scenes, and life-sized Santas in sleds with reindeer in full flight. Flotillas of exuberant elves and masses of gingerbread men crowd each other right up to the property lines. This is Christmas cheer on steroids.

You'll find the most elaborately decorated homes between 79th and 86th Streets, between 11th and 13th Avenues. The indispensable block: 84th between 12th and 13th, where one home, sign-posted "Santa's House," features a row of elves making nutcrackers, Mrs. Claus rocking in her chair, and a smiling, waving Winnie-the-Pooh. Across the street is a colonnaded-mansion in front of which toy soldiers twelve-feet high slowly stride in unison, while around them life-size dancing figures cavort in peasant fustian. Over on 82nd Street at No. 1054 Santa sits in the picture window, tickling the ivories of a grand piano. At 86th Street and Twelfth Avenue more massive wooden soldiers await. By the end of your drive, you might feel a little Scrooge-like for getting away with only a tree and the odd sprig of holly around the living room.

Afterwards, take everybody out for old-fashioned Italian food, including highly regarded Sicilian-style pizza, at **L&B Spumoni Gardens**, a family-style restaurant at 2725 86th Street (718-372-8400).

P.S. A car is best for this, but you can take the B train to 79th Street or Eighth Avenue and do it on foot. Bring trail mix.

D.I.Y. Christmas Trees

On almost any New York street corner from the end of November until Christmas Eve, you'll find someone cute from Vermont who has gorgeous, fragrant trees for sale. Despite having these benign outlanders on hand, many New Yorkers feel a visceral need to journey into deepest New Jersey to find a Christmas tree to cut down themselves (or to be cut down while they watch). Here are three of the very best from the Garden State:

At **Hidden Hollow Farm**, in Warren County, you'll find an old farmhouse and more than 20,000 trees to choose from (as well as wreaths, gifts, etc.). The highlight: actual oxen to pull your chosen tree back from the field!

- **Hidden Hollow Farm**, *18 Spring Lane, Washington, N.J. Call 908-689-5678 for directions. Visit www.njskylands.com for more information.*
- **Glenview Farm** in Blairstown (also Warren County) has high-quality trees and great views from atop a mountain ridge. You'll be offered hot chocolate and cookies.
- **Glenview Farm**, 2 Glenview Lane, Blairstown, NJ. Visit www.glenviewfarm.com for a map and more information.

Further west in Phillipsburg, about sixty miles from Manhattan, is the aptly named **Perfect Christmas Tree Farm**. The farmhouse is an old stone beauty with a roaring fire in its kitchen hearth; the farmer has grown trees from seed for over sixty years. With its hayrides and serious gift shop, this is a very appealing place, but take note: the trees have already been cut.

- **Perfect Christmas Tree Farm**, *999 U.S. Route 22, Phillipsburg, N.J. Visit www.perfectchristmastree.com for a map and more information.*

Finally, there's an extremely special place for the very young just up the Hudson, in Newburgh, New York. **Lawrence Farms Orchards** has horse-and-carriage rides, a bakery, home-made preserves, and best of all, an enchanting little play village decorated with Christmas lights.

- **Lawrence Farms Orchards**, *Frozen Ridge Road, Newburgh, NY. Go to www.lawrencefarmsorchards.com for pictures, a map, and more information.*

New York Turtle and Tortoise Society Annual Show

If you're contemplating buying one of those silver-dollar-sized turtles you saw for sale in Chinatown (see p. 18), why not attend this show, held every spring (usually early June) in a school playground in the West Village? You'll see just how imposing your little green friend might become. And if you're simply curious about these mysterious charmers, you won't be disappointed. Some of the more gigantic beasts roam free, munching on stuff; others lie snug as kittens against their owners' chests; everywhere turtle-lovers are enthusiastically swapping tips about health, hygiene, and diet. This placid scene is a sweet example of the eccentricities of the human heart.

- **Annual Turtle and Tortoise Show**, *held at Village Community School, 272 W. 10th St. at Washington St., www.nytts.org.*

Clearwater Festival

On Father's Day weekend, when you're looking for something special to do, take the car and drive up to Croton-on-Hudson to Clearwater's **Great Hudson River Revival**. For more than thirty years, folk singer and environmentalist Pete Seeger has presided over this joyful celebration of the Hudson River and its delicate eco-system. It's become so successful that up to 15,000 people are likely to show up, which makes it the country's largest annual environmental celebration. No need to worry, though. Big as it is, the festival manages to retain its relaxed, old-timey and welcoming feel. It happens over two days in Croton Point Park, right on the river. There are several stages where you can hear distinguished performers like Buffy Sainte-Marie or Paul Winter and every kind of music from zydeco and jazz to opera. You can sample ethnic foods, buy crafts, and browse various environmental exhibits. For the children, there's a special area with crafts and activities, a children's stage, and, at every turn, storytellers, jugglers, clowns, magicians, and mimes. That venerable sprite, Pete Seeger himself, may even be found behind a microphone somewhere. Go, have fun, and do something to save our waters.

- **Great Hudson River Revival**, *Croton Point Park, Croton-on-Hudson, Westchester. Visit www.clearwater.org/revival for details.*

cityscapes:
all around the town

You Must Take the N train (to Queens)

Isamu Noguchi Museum...Socrates Sculpture Park...Museum of the Moving Image...good eats: Uncle George's, Tierras Colombianas, Omonia Café, and more.

Isamu Noguchi Museum

Two specialized museums and one invigorating riverside sculpture park—all of them very appealing to kids—make this relatively small area of Queens worth several visits.

Pick a nice day, because you'll be walking around. Start by taking the N train to Broadway in Astoria, then walk west toward Vernon Boulevard and the East River. The dense commercial traffic gives way to residential streets, then to warehouses. At Vernon, turn left and walk a block to 33rd Road. Look carefully up 33rd and you will see that the nondescript gray building that faces Vernon isn't so nondescript after all.

Sculptor Isamu Noguchi established his studio here in the 1960s, in order to be close to the marble suppliers then operating along Vernon Boulevard. When he turned the place into a museum, he was careful not to disrupt the building's continuity with its surroundings. The result is perhaps the most hidden-away museum in the city, as well as one of the most serene.

Here you'll find almost 300 works in stone, wood, and clay, including sculptures, lamps, and project models. The work, spare and abstract, is very accessible to children. The effects of the imposing stone pieces in the ground-floor studio often hinge on simple oppositions like hollow and filled; smooth and round; heavy and light.

In the garden, seek out a piece called *The Well (Variation on a Tsukubai)*, an interpretation of the traditional Japanese fountain, or tsukubai, as a massive stone cube from which water flows so quietly and smoothly that the stone seems sheathed in glass. Like many other works here, it's so tactile you'll want to reach out and touch it. Resist the temptation; touching is not permitted because, as a guide explained to us, the natural oils in our hands are bad for the stone. Tell the children not to take umbrage—a very different museum is just a short walk away.

Return to Vernon Boulevard, turn right, walk two blocks or so north and you'll see **Socrates Sculpture Park**, almost five acres of not-at-all-manicured shorefront dotted with pieces of contemporary sculpture, some quite large, all set against views of the river, Roosevelt Island, and the Upper East Side. Founded in 1986 by a group of artists and locals led by sculptor Mark di Suvero as an informal gallery for local artists, the park has been bought by the city, which put up a plaque and, fortunately, left it at that.

Today it is the only place in the city specifically intended for the creation and display of large-scale art works, and one of the most unusual picnic spots in town. The art here changes twice a year and its quality varies widely. But Socrates Park has a feature that lifts it above all competition for kids' interest: Nothing on display here is off-limits. The pieces can all be touched, sat on, ridden, rubbed, or run around. Indeed, many seem designed for hands-on use. In past visits, we've seen children climb on an enormous green tree snake, trot around a caged-in catwalk surrounding four saplings, enter a steep brick amphitheater built inside a hill, or buddy up to a trio of larger-than-life teenagers on pedestals. We've picnicked on a squishy-looking sofa made of mosaic tile.

Socrates Sculpture Park is open 365 days a year from 10 a.m. until sunset. During July and August, movies are shown on Wednesday nights, and there are other special events throughout the year.

A short distance away, but probably the main event of another trip, is the **Museum of the Moving Image (MoMI)**, which is so much fun to visit, you might forget how much serious historic paraphernalia is here. Artifacts include Muybridge movement studies and makeup samples from *Planet of the Apes*. The core exhibit, *Behind the Screen*, explores the intricacies of producing and showing movies and televison. In Tut's Fever Movie Palace, a tiny (36 seats), riotously kitschy movie theater designed by Red Grooms, the kids can watch old-time serials with titles like *Panther Girl from the Kongo*.

For most kids, the absolute highlight will be the hands-on video game exhibit. The legendary games of long ago are all here: *Donkey Kong*, *Pac-Man*, and such cult classics as *Star Wars*, *Karate Champ*, *Pole Position*, and *Space Invaders*. Most are in working order; each has a card explaining its role in the saga of computer-operated entertainment. You'll use a lot of change, but save some for the gift shop. It's a good one: not just the usual logo mugs, T-shirts, and caps, but also posters, fridge magnets, claymation sets, and lunch bags of undeniable adorability.

Near MoMI is the heart of New York's most Greek neighborhood. Try **Uncle George's**, which looks like your standard coffee shop—except for the lamb roasting on a spit in the window and the more-esoteric-than-usual Greek specialties on the lengthy menu. Nearby, but an ethnic world away, is **Tierras Colombianas**, where you can get rice and beans, fried chicken, and other Latin specialties that small mouths enjoy. Wherever you go, save room for dessert and the **Omonia Café** on the corner of Broadway and 33rd Street. Here, you can drink serious coffee and sample rice pudding while the children put away lavish sundaes or gaudy, sticky cakes—a favorite is all chocolate, topped with an icing mouse.

- **Isamu Noguchi Museum**, *9–01 33rd Rd. at Vernon Blvd., Queens, 718-204-7088, www.noguchi.org.*
- **Socrates Sculpture Park**, *Broadway at the East River, 718-956-1819, Queens, www.socratessculpturepark.org.*
- **Museum of the Moving Image**, *Fifth Ave. at 36th St., Queens, 718-784-0077, www.movingimage.us.*
- **Uncle George's Greek Tavern**, *33–19 Broadway at 34th St., Queens, 718-626-0593.*
- **Tierras Colombianas**, *33–01 Broadway at 33rd St., Queens, 718-956-3012.*
- **Omonia Café**, *3220 Broadway at 33rd St., Queens, 718-274-6650.*
- **Getting there:**
  Noguchi Museum and Socrates Sculpture Park: N train to Broadway. On weekends, the museum runs a shuttle bus that picks up passengers on Park Ave. and 70th St. in front of the Asia Society. Call or visit the website for

information.

For Museum of the Moving Image: R, V, or G to Steinway Street. Head south on Steinway, then right on Fifth Ave. to the corner of 36 St.; N or W to Broadway (Astoria), east to 36th St., turn right, continue two blocks to Fifth Ave.

Hallowed Ground: The World Trade Center and Environs

WTC Tribute Center...St. Paul's Chapel...Double Check...Company 10 Firehouse... FDNY Memorial Wall...views of the site...Winter Garden respite.

While Ground Zero has become one of our city's most popular tourist destinations, it's also a place many New Yorkers prefer to avoid. Built, along with the World Financial Center and Battery Park City, on some of the world's most expensive landfill, the World Trade Center was, literally, an awesome sight.

The vast construction pit it has become is also awesome, both in scale and in the gravity of its atmosphere. If your kids are old enough to understand what they're seeing and more importantly if you're all up for it, this is a deeply moving place to visit, and a fascinating one. There is no other New York neighborhood in which our city's oldest past and most recent present coexist so dramatically. The site itself is a work in progress whose final form is still undecided. It is constantly changing and will continue to do so for years to come.

On Liberty Street, past the ominous, black-shrouded Deutsche Bank, is the **WTC Tribute Center**, which houses five galleries that take you chronologically from the Towers' construction, through 9/11, its aftermath, and plans for the future. The exhibit contains sights and sounds that may be difficult for some children—and some adults—to take. The Tribute Center also conducts tours of the site, all led by individuals who were present at the time of the attack or involved later in rescue and recovery efforts. They are invariably sympathetic and well-informed.

You can get a sense of this haunting place on your own, however. Start at **St. Paul's Chapel**, a small house of worship completed in 1766 and separated from Ground Zero by nothing more than a narrow street and its modest graveyard. Miraculously, it survived the attack completely intact; not one pane of glass was broken.

For nine months thereafter, St. Paul's was the principal refuge for workers on the pile, a place for meals, massage, and rest. Fifteen thousand teddy bears were given away to those involved in rescue and recovery. The iron fence outside the chapel and the pews inside became encrusted with notes, photos, banners, ribbons, children's drawings—an ad hoc memorial of stunning power and eloquence.

Today, arcs of wooden chairs face into the center of the simple, pastel-painted chapel. Around the room are displays of memorabilia, discreet video installations, photographs, and quotes from veterans of those months. There's a mockup of the cooking area, complete with a handwritten recipe for chicken stew and instructions for its preparation. A placard beside George Washington's pew—in which he prayed before his presidential inauguration—notes that it was used for foot massage and other podiatric therapies, "as many of Washington's troops fought at Valley Forge without boots, many saw placing the podiatry station in this pew as a fitting tribute." There's a sample cot and a rolling clothes-rack draped with hundreds of origami peace cranes from Japan. It's a dignified and spiritual place, so much so that tears may come.

Don't leave without visiting the graveyard, which contains headstones dating from the eighteenth century. London plane trees arch overhead. It's beautiful and contemplative, and directly across the street is Ground Zero itself. The site is surrounded by chicken wire swathed in green fabric, so you can't see much, but enormous cranes tower above and throngs of people from all over the world mill around.

Walk down Church Street to Liberty. In the pedestrian plaza on the southeast corner, you'll see *Double Check*, J. Seward Johnson Jr.'s life-size bronze of a man in a suit sitting on a bench. After 9/11, the statue was found lying on its side, knocked free of its original site and covered in ash, but still intact. People occasionally leave sandwiches, flowers, or notes in his open attaché case.

West of the Tribute Center on Liberty is the **Company 10 Firehouse**, which lost six men that day. The firemen here are exceptionally warm and smiley, posing for pictures and joking with the tourists. On the west wall of the firehouse is the **FDNY Memorial Wall**, a bronze frieze of firefighters at the site, smoke and flames billowing from the towers, and the names of all 343 fireman lost on the day listed below. Continuing down Liberty Street, the names of all the victims are listed on big green placards attached to the wire fence.

At the bottom of Liberty, climb the stairs to the South Bridge (a.k.a. the Liberty Street Bridge), where you can take in the first of the two best views of the site, with its slurry walls and covered tracks of the PATH train snaking into the station.

Walking down cool marbled corridors, follow the signs to the **Winter Garden**, passing the other remarkably clear view. Soon you'll see the familiar sweeping flight of stairs that lead down to the towering palm trees and the view of the Hudson beyond. It's hard to believe this beautiful space lay in ruins. Descend the stairs, go to the **Ciao Bella Café** store on the left of the piazza and buy some fabulous ice cream. Take it outside, sit at a spindly table and absorb the view: rollerbladers, tourists, seagulls, yachts bobbing in the water. Talk, think, or just look. It's a well-earned respite.

Note: The WTC is close to some other attractions for the historically minded. Just north of the site and even further west is the **Irish Hunger Memorial**. It doesn't have much in the way of explanation, but this small rocky hillside (which includes stones from each Irish county, the crumbled walls of an Irish cottage, and native Irish plants) seems to float evocatively above the street. A few blocks east is the new **African Burial Ground National Monument** on Reade Street and Broadway, dedicated in 2007 to the memory of the 20,000 or more Africans interred in this ground between 1629 and 1794.

- **WTC Tribute Visitor Center**, *120 Liberty St., bet. Greenwich and Church Sts., on the south side of Ground Zero, 866-737-1184, 212-393-9160 ext. 138, www.trib-*

utenyc.org. *(The Company 10 Firehouse is next door.)*

- **St. Paul's Chapel**, *209 Broadway at Church St., bet. Fulton and Vesey Sts., 212-233-4164, www.saint-paulschapel.org.*
- **Ciao Bella Café**: *World Financial Center, 212-786-4707, www.ciaobellagelato.com.*
- **Irish Hunger Memorial**, *corner of Vesey St. and North End Ave., www.batteryparkcity.org.*
- **African Burial Ground National Monument**, *Reade St., east of 290 Broadway, www.nps.gov/afbg.*
- **Getting there:** *2 or 3 train to Park Place; 1, 9, 4, 5, or A to Fulton St./Broadway Nassau; 6 to Brooklyn Bridge/City Hall; E to Chambers; R to Cortlandt or Rector Sts.; PATH train to World Trade Center Station.*

Where the Money Is: Financial District
Stock Exchange...Federal Reserve Bank of New York... fast, fast food...art on Mammon's turf...The Cunard Building...Trinity Church...shopping...dinner at Odeon.

This weekday tour is strictly for older kids and it requires some advance planning, but it's worth it.

The New York Stock Exchange has been, alas, closed to visitors since 9/11. However, you can take your teen to the spanking new location of the **Museum of American Financial History**. It's in a 1928 building that formerly housed the Bank of New York and, like so many of these palaces of finance, it has a jaw-droppingly ornate banking hall and spectacular murals. The permanent collection contains a haunting sepia photograph of Wall Street—the first-ever!—taken from a ship, as well as historic documents of all kinds, including a U.S. Treasury Bond issued to George Washington with the first known use of the dollar sign (wow!) and a ticker tape from the grim morning of October 29, 1929.

If your child has a real interest in the world's financial workings, book a tour of the **Federal Reserve Bank of New York**, just a few blocks away at the junction of Liberty and Wall. This imposing place actually issues currency, and houses more gold than

Fort Knox—five floors of it, owned by many different nations. In the old days, international transactions used to be marked here by physical transfer, from one area to another. Yes, they do let you see the gold. Keep in mind that the minimum age for the tour is sixteen and reservations must be booked a month in advance, an inconvenience that only adds to its appeal.

If you're hungry by now, you're in luck. This area is fast-food central. Up and down the narrow streets are burger joints, pizzerias, etc. (The idea is to snack early for the sake of an early dinner that's special.) Fortified, you can take an art breather outside. Start with Louise Nevelson's **Shadows and Flags**, a sculptural installation in the plaza in front of the Federal Reserve. Look up from the middle of the seven jagged forms— they're designed to be viewed that way—and then cross the street, into the lower level of Chase Manhattan Plaza. You're facing a plate glass window, behind which is a characteristically discreet and meditative Noguchi work, a sunken garden with black rocks and lapping water. Walk past a striking car fender sculpture on the wall (**Triptych** by Jason Seeley) to the escalator, which will take you up to the outdoor plaza containing Dubuffet's wonderfully idiosyncratic **Group of Four Trees**. These looming black-and-white oddities, more mushroomy than treelike, are a charming surprise here in the stuffy ambience of high finance.

Walk across Wall Street or Exchange Place to Broadway. Look down toward the Battery to get a sense of the small scale of old New York. Many of the buildings around here have gorgeous lobbies and architectural details. **The Cunard Building** (now a post office) at 25 Broadway, where you'd go to book passage on the Lusitania, has an incredible painted ceiling, as well as murals and frescoes. Now walk up to formidable **Trinity Church**, one of the city's richest institutions, rebuilt in its third incarnation to dominate Wall Street. (Literally—it looms up in front of you as you walk up Wall Street.) Buried in the churchyard here are Alexander Hamilton and Robert Fulton (of steamboat fame). By the way, it was because Africans were not permitted to be buried here that the Reade Street burial ground (see p. 83) came into being.

Having seen where so much money is made, perhaps you're in the mood to spend some. Along Park Place, occupying several storefronts, sits the indispensable **J&R**, a neighborhood stalwart that weathered severe damage and then vastly reduced business after 9/11 to remain a technogeek's paradise. J&R has cds, dvds, and electronic tackle of every type, as well as knowledgeable staff to advise. Nearby, **Tents & Trails** also endured 9/11 and its difficult aftermath to reclaim its place as New York's foremost outdoor equipment shop, with competitive prices and personnel, many of them outdoors-folk themselves, who know their stuff. Further west, directly across the street from Ground Zero (see p. 81), is **Century 21**, the city's best discount department store, chockablock with incredible bargains. Calvin Klein undies, anyone?

You're probably ready for a drink and dinner. What better place than **Odeon** on West Broadway? It's enduringly cool and mellow, the young are welcomed and the food is as beguiling as the atmosphere. We strongly advise that you pick the crème brûlée for dessert.

- **Museum of American Financial History**, *48 Wall St., at Hanover St., 212-908-4110, www.financialhistory.org.*
- **Federal Reserve Bank**, *33 Liberty St. at Maiden Ln., 212-720-6130, www.ny.frb.org.*
- **Louise Nevelson Plaza**, *William and Liberty Sts.*
- **Noguchi and Dubuffet**, *1 Chase Manhattan Plaza at Cedar St.*
- **Cunard Building**, *U.S. Post Office (Bowling Green), 25 Broadway bet. Beaver St. and Exchange Pl.*
- **Trinity Church**, *Broadway at Wall St., 212-602-0872, www.trinitywallstreet.org.*
- **J&R**, *23 Park Row (across from City Hall Park), 212-238-9000, www.jr.com.*
- **Tents & Trails**, *21 Park Pl. (near Church St.), 212-227-1760, www.tenttrails.com.*
- **Century 21**, *22 Cortlandt St., bet. Broadway and Church Sts., 212-227-9092, www.c21stores.com.*
- **Odeon**, *145 W. Broadway, at Thomas St., 212-233-0507,*

www.theodeonrestaurant.com.
- **Getting there:** *4, 5, or 6 to Brooklyn Bridge; N or R to City Hall.*

Two Boroughs, One Majestic Bridge

Ruben's Empanadas...South Street Seaport...Pier 17...world's most beautiful bridge...DUMBO parks, play-grounds, views...a carousel...Half Pint Toys...Jacques Torres Chocolate...Bubby's...Grimaldi's Pizzeria...Brooklyn Ice Cream Factory.

This trip requires a lovely weekend day (you don't want chilly gusts off the river to buffet the smallest member).

Manhattan side

Fuel up with a flaky, savory breakfast empanada at **Ruben's** on Fulton Street. They have bacon-and-egg as well as the tradi-tional spinach, meat, and chicken versions of these savory pat-ties. Then head down to the **South Street Seaport**, which, despite the fact that it's becoming a hub for high-priced chain stores, is invigorating and full of nice surprises.

One not-at-all-surprising aspect is the multitude of street performers: lots of white painted, motionless people-statues; contortionists, magicians, skateboarders. It's actually festive and fun. Stroll the old streets like Cannon's Walk and Schermerhorn Row, soaking up remnants of nineteenth-centu-ry port ambience. There are Federal-era buildings on Peck Slip, between Water and Front Streets, some sliding into decrepi-tude. The oldest is No. 273 Water Street, once the house/store that retired sea captain Joseph Rose built for himself in 1773.

At the Visitors' Center at 209 Water Street, buy a ticket that will admit you to the South Street Seaport Museum and its eight historic ships, including the venerable Peking, a cargo vessel built in 1911. (On board there's a flickery short film of the Peking fighting a storm.) Don't miss the Walter Lord Gallery, which features one of the world's great collections of ocean liner models, from the tiny to the hugely spectacular. The enor-mous model of the Queen Mary 1, made in 1942, has a minute

Winston Churchill on deck, facing the wrong way (something to do with the logistical demands of getting the model into the space). The Queen of Bermuda is a "half-model," which means that the back is a cross-section showing the inside of the ship. The detail is amazing. Look for the two swimming pools, the stable of racehorses on their ways to the islands, the barbershop, and (hooray!) a naked person taking a shower. The Seaport has masses of childrens' activities and special events, from Fire Day to the Festival of Maritime Work and Culture. (Call in advance to see what's on the docket.) As your kids drag you to **Pier 17**, peer into the Maritime Craft Center and see artisans at work carving and building model boats.

Pier 17 isn't much different from an over-crowded, tacky mall anywhere in the country—except for the fact that it has a killer view of the **Brooklyn Bridge** from the third-floor food court (be warned: there is a lavish candy store up there, too). The kids will probably be drawn lemming-like to the many novelty stores specializing in everything from purple merchandise (Purpleicious) to jewels to protect you from the evil eye (Angel Eye). The souvenir we recommend has nothing to do with New York but it's gorgeous: a single butterfly in a lucite cube for $15 (don't worry, store literature emphasizes that it has lived out its entire life-cycle) from Mariposa.

Brooklyn Bridge to Brooklyn

The kids may tell you that they "went from school," but what the heck, take them anyway. Make it a regular thing! To get onto the bridge from the Manhattan side, cross the street from City Hall and start up the walkway. It's magnificent up there, but scary too, with the wind whistling through the cables and the traffic buzzing below. Hang on to the tinies, who should have a hat or scarf to protect their ears from the ever-present wind. Before going, you could read up on the history a little (David McCullough's *The Great Bridge* is marvelous) so that you can give the kids a sense of the engineers' achievements and the odd gruesome detail (twenty involved in the bridge's construction died, most from the bends, including its designer, John Roebling). Coming down off the bridge (first exit to your left,

left at the bottom of the stairs, and then left again), you find yourself in:

DUMBO: The neighborhood "Down Under the Manhattan Bridge Overpass" is fascinating, compact, and satisfyingly easy to visit. To understand its appeal, go to the foot of Old Fulton Street, facing The River Café and Manhattan. Turn right along Water Street, under the Brooklyn Bridge, then take the first left down to the water. On your left is a sweeping cobble-stoned expanse that wraps around the anchorage of the bridge, and from it you can see what is, in our humble opinion, the city's best view—past the Seaport, past Wall Street's towers and canyons, past the Statue of Liberty and Governor's Island and out into the harbor. A boat or two will sidle by; the water will lap at the pilings, and chances are, you'll realize you've seen this view before in some of the umpteen ads and commercials that have been staged here.

Across the street is the **Empire-Fulton Ferry State Park**, a grassy and hilly place with Civil War-era warehouses abutting it, great for a picnic. It's also an anchor of the thrilling work-in-progress that is the **Brooklyn Bridge Park**. This long-overdue transformation of decrepit waterfront acreage into a sweeping stretch of green goes, in this direction, as far as the Manhattan Bridge (and is planned to go on up to Queens). The completed piece is spectacular, with a very spiffy nautical-themed playground, a pebble shore, a rocky cove that contains a small sandy beach, and, as you approach the south side of the Manhattan Bridge, a view of the towering bridge—its trains and traffic—will make you gape. Who ever thought the Manhattan Bridge could be so beautiful?

Away from the water, the streets are great for exploring. At 56 Water Street, you can see (but not ride) a glorious **carousel** dating from 1922 that was rescued from a defunct amusement park in Ohio. Jane Walentas, artist-wife of the man responsible for the development of DUMBO, has lovingly restored it for over twenty-two years and promises that it will at some point be placed in Brooklyn Bridge Park. Also on Water Street is the original **Jacques Torres Chocolate**, a palace of delights for chocolate lovers big and small. Wander into the fancy kid's clothing/toy store called **Half Pint** and check out the menu at **Bubby's**. The DUMBO branch of this beloved comfort food emporium occupies a roomy, light-filled space with great views.

If you want the real Brooklyn experience, though, you should stop in at **Grimaldi's**, a renowned old-style pizzeria up Old Fulton Street. Pictures of Frank Sinatra adorn the walls, his tunes are on the jukebox, and the waiters are expert at swinging between the crowded tables without stepping on errant three-year-olds. The fabulous pizza is the real thing—fresh mozzarella, homemade tomato sauce, and delicate smoky crust—with no goat cheese or radicchio to ruin it for the children. (They do not sell individual slices, though the eponymous Mr. Grimaldi himself does, elsewhere in Brooklyn—see p. 103.) This place is very popular, especially at kid-time (5:30 on), but the line moves steadily, so stick with it.

Afterwards, stroll down to the water again, this time to Fulton Ferry Landing, between Bargemusic and The River Café. This is the site of a ferry that from 1814 until the 1960s connected Lower Manhattan and the borough of Brooklyn. Now it's a wide wooden deck with little benches and a wrought-iron fence with inscriptions from Walt Whitman, who lived close by. Some weekends, it seems that every Brooklyn wedding party has come down here for a photo-op. **The Brooklyn Ice Cream Factory** is in the renovated Fireboat House, serving a small but scrumptious selection of homemade ice cream delights, which are perfect for slurping while watching the brides and grooms. Finally, flag down a taxi leaving The River Cafe and take it to the subway, or splurge and take it all the way home.

Manhattan Side

- **Ruben's Empanadas**, *64 Fulton St. near the Seaport, 212-962-5330.*
- **South Street Seaport Museum and Visitors' Center**, *209 Water St., 212-748-8600. For information on family programs, call 212-748-8758, www.southstseaport.org.*
- **Getting there:** *2, 3, 4, or 5 train to Fulton St.; A or C to Broadway/Nassau. Walk east on Fulton St. to Water St.*

Brooklyn Side

- **Empire-Fulton Ferry State Park** and **Brooklyn Bridge Park**, *check www.brooklynbridgepark.org for events and updates.*
- **Jane's Carousel**, *56 Water St., at Williams St., is open on weekend afternoons.*
- **Jacques Torres Chocolate**, *66 Water St., at Williams St., 718-875-9772, www.mrchocolate.com.*
- **Half Pint**, *55 Washington St., at Rector St., 718-875-4007, www.halfpintstore.com.*
- **Bubby's**, *1 Main St., 718-222-0666, www.bubbys.com.*
- **Grimaldi's Pizza**, *19 Old Fulton St., bet. Water and Front Sts., 718-858-4300.*
- **Brooklyn Ice Cream Factory** *at Fulton Ferry Landing Pier, 718-246-3963.*
- **Getting home:** *A at High St.*

Village People and Places
*Union Square Greenmarket...The Forbes Galleries...
Washington Square...little houses, little streets...
a restaurant with a thing for cowgirls.*

The Village can be hard for kids—too crowded, too much architecture and history, too many serious restaurants. This jaunt, preferably undertaken on a bustling Saturday, makes it fun and easy.

Start at the **Union Square Greenmarket**, so that the children can fuel up with a little bottle of fancy juice and pretzels, muffins, or the chocolate chip cookies from **Wilklow Farm**, which, in addition to being large, have the appropriate ratio of chips to cookie.

Stroll down Broadway. If you're feeling expansive, stop in at **Forbidden Planet** and spend a few minutes amid the pasty science-fiction fanatics while your children pick over the comics, figures, games, and posters. Then go down to 12th Street and west to Fifth to **The Forbes Galleries**.

This place is a joy. Malcolm Forbes never put away childish

things. On the contrary, he collected and cherished them, and much of his collection is on show here—but it's the toy soldiers and boats that you're here to see. The first gallery contains 500 toy ships and boats of all sizes and degrees of complexity, deployed in tableaux on gleaming glass seas. All around, you hear jolly nautical band music and the booming of ships' horns. The submarine display is the real kid-pleaser; the subs float murkily behind a long vertical window, you hear the ominous beeping of depth finders, and suddenly you notice the Lusitania, sprawled on the bottom.

In the next gallery, there are more than 10,000 toy soldiers and other figures set up in pitched battles and other arrangements. Aztecs fight Cortéz's conquistadors; tiny wounded soldiers suffer in field hospitals; Indians on a moving belt circle a wagon train, and regiment after regiment march on parade. (Be warned: Some of these tableaux are, incomprehensibly, installed too high up for small children. So you may have to hoist the kids up from time to time, or locate the stool that's usually somewhere around.)

Further on, William Tell prepares his bow to shoot the apple from his son's head. Peer through a little porthole-shaped window in a room called Land of Counterpane, and you can pretend to be the child of Robert Louis Stevenson's poem, with all your soldiers laid out in formation on the bed in front of you.

Then wander down Fifth to ever-raffish **washington square** where, if you're lucky, you'll find a pleasantly ramshackle assortment of buskers, magicians, and mimes—some of whom may be talented (this is where Philippe Petit, the noted high-wire artist, used to perform).

Now begins the most Villagey aspect of the tour: Bleecker Street which, despite its many upscale shops and tawdry tourist joints, retains some flavor of its bohemian past. There are still funky record stores, bakeries, and lovely old cafés with tin ceilings. West of Sixth Avenue, you'll hit some enticing food shops—**Rocco's Pastry Shop** and **Murray's Cheese**, as well as the legendary **John's**, still serving its pizza of the gods. At Seventh Avenue, turn south and head for some of New York's oldest, prettiest blocks. Of course, they look familiar; you've seen them in countless movies.

Turn right on St. Luke's Place to Hudson Street, then up Morton Street, then left again onto Bedford. Here, you'll find No. 75 1/2, a house, that is not merely New York's narrowest (9 1/2 ft.), but was also inhabited at one time or another by Edna St. Vincent Millay, William Steig, Margaret Mead, John Barrymore, and Cary Grant. Walk west down L-shaped Commerce Street to the Cherry Lane Theater. Commerce dead-ends at Barrow; turn right, back toward Seventh, cross Bedford, and you'll see on your left a mysterious little stone courtyard. Walk in. Ahead of you is a forbidding, heavily barred door with no sign. This is **Chumley's**.

If the stars are in alignment, the former speakeasy that became a convivial bar and literary hangout will be back in business after a nasty incident in 2007 when construction caused an interior wall to collapse and the bar was temporarily (we hope) closed. It has framed book jackets on the walls, a world-class jukebox (rivaled only by the one in the Corner Bistro on West 4th Street), and a roaring log fire. (The food here is good enough and children are allowed to eat here, by the way.)

Exit via Chumley's rear entrance onto Bedford (another door without a sign), and turn right until you hit Grove Street. At the corner, gape awhile at Twin Peaks, a truly eccentric house at 102 Bedford, and at the tiny frame cottage in front of it. Then make a left and keep walking until you see another secret place—Grove Court, a perfect row of six small red houses dating from 1854, tucked away in their private courtyard.

Surfeited on architecture, the children need rewards in the form of food. There are masses of places to choose from—the **Elephant and Castle** on Greenwich Avenue for simple fare beautifully prepared, John's for pizza, and any number of taquerias and cafés.

Our favorite kid-friendly restaurant around here is **Cowgirl** on Hudson Street. This is not one of those mass-produced margaritas-from-a-mix "concept restaurants." On the contrary, it's the personal expression of Sherry Delamarter, who is obsessed with all things Western. There's a little museum in there, and a mock Western living room with a painted night sky above the roof beams; there are glass-fronted displays of barbed wire, tied by the great barbed-wire tiers of the Old West (who knew there were such people?). This is definitely one woman's vision; it's wildly appealing and the sustaining Western-cum-Southwestern food is good. The children's menu has burgers and dogs, but also a single cheese enchilada and Frito pie made in the bag. On your way out, investigate the campy little gift shop, which has candy, water-guns in holsters, beaded belts, and bandannas. Keep this friendly place in mind for birthday parties, too.

P.S. The *Sex and the City* aspect: If you haven't already been to the **Magnolia Bakery**, this may be the time for a box of the pastel-iced, breathtakingly sweet cupcakes beloved by Carrie and her pals. If your family includes a fan of the show, trek over to 66 Perry, between Bleecker and West 4th, for a look at Carrie's stoop. Please resist the urge to pose for pictures on the steps—it's definitely not cool, since real people live there!

- **Union Square Greenmarket**, *Union Square West and 17th St., www.cenyc.org.*
- **Forbidden Planet**, *840 Broadway at 13th St., 212-473-1576, www.fpnyc.com.*
- **The Forbes Galleries**, *62 Fifth Ave. at 12th St., 212-206-5548, www.forbesgalleries.com*
- **Rocco's Pastry Shop**, *243 Bleecker St., bet. Leroy and Carmine Sts., 212-242-6031, www.roccospastry.com.*
- **Murray's Cheese**, *254 Bleecker St., bet. Leroy and Morton Sts., 212-243-3289, www.murrayscheese.com.*
- **John's of Bleecker**, *278 Bleecker St., bet. 6th and 7th Aves., 212-243-1680.*
- **Chumley's Restaurant**, *86 Bedford St., bet. Barrow and Grove Sts., 212-675-4449.*
- **Elephant and Castle**, *68 Greenwich Ave. at W. 11th St., 212-243-1400, www.elephantandcastle.com.*
- **Cowgirl**, *519 Hudson St. at 10th St., 212-633-1133, www.cowgirlnyc.com.*
- **Magnolia Bakery**, *401 Bleecker St., corner of W. 11th St.*
- **Getting there:** *4, 5, 6, L, N, Q, R, or W to Union Sq.*

On the Waterfront: Red Hook

*Beard Street Pier art shows...Summer Arts Festival...
Hudson Waterfront Museum...great Key lime pie and cupcakes...fierce soccer and the best street food in town.*

Red Hook is a great place to take the kids—however surprising
that may sound to people who remember it as a forlorn and
crime-ridden remnant of the old waterfront, which was not,
after all, very long ago.

Today, with its space and light, cobblestone streets and
nineteenth-century warehouses, Red Hook can feel a world
away from the rest of New York City. It's resurgent, too, bustling
with artists and urban pioneers who've come to live and work
at the water's edge. Shoppers from outlying precincts come to
the new Fairway and Ikea stores, and Red Hook's modest brick
houses are being snapped up for big bucks. Even the Queen
Mary 2 docks here! Most importantly for us, there are a couple
of summer attractions that your children will love.

Time your visit for a weekend that coincides with one of
the **art shows** held by the Brooklyn Waterfront Artists Coalition
(BWAC) at the Beard Street Pier. Walk or take the bus all the
way down Van Brunt Street to the pier where, in a cavernous
and darkly atmospheric warehouse, you'll find art that's innova-
tive, colorful, and often downright weird–in other words, fascinating to the young. If you go on the opening weekend of the
Annual Pier Show, you'll be dancing on the cobblestones to a
live band. There's also a breathtaking view out over the water.
Lady Liberty! Ferries! Tugs, barges, merchant ships! Ducks!

Summer unofficially begins in these parts with the **Red
Hook Waterfront Arts Festival** in June. It features music,
dance, and spoken word performances, screenings, workshops,
and assorted kid-friendly amusements—all free and all imbued
with a marked and well-deserved sense of local pride. Maybe
when you go, the Queen Mary 2 will be docked nearby at the
Brooklyn Cruise Terminal at Pier 12. (You can't miss it!)

A block away, moored to the garden pier at the end of
Conover Street, sits the little red Lehigh Valley Barge 79, home

of the **Hudson Waterfront Museum** and, every June, the **Circus Sundays** program. Inside the barge, the weathered space is small and redolent with history; assorted nautical artifacts are casually displayed while performers—new vaudevillians, jugglers, clowns, etc.,—connect easily with their audience. It's an intimate little space, and thrillingly close to the Statue of Liberty.

A couple of blocks away at Pier 41 on Van Dyke Street is the home of **Steve's Authentic Key Lime Pies**. Steve is a Floridian-turned-Brooklynite who ships fresh key limes to his bakery for pies so scrumptiously tart and custardy that they're sold all over town, from Peter Luger's to Zabar's. You'll probably want to take home a pie or three, but for on-site snacking, consider the swingle, a small, chocolate-covered key-lime pie on a stick. Alternatively, or perhaps afterwards, head over to the locally-beloved **Baked** for the dense red velvet cupcake with cinnamon buttercream icing. Or save the pie and/or cake for dessert and do a trendy cool thing—eating at the **Red Hook ballfields**. On weekend afternoons from May to October, ferociously competitive soccer games take place here and along Bay and Clinton Streets food vendors prepare and sell a wide variety of Latin American and Caribbean dishes. This is consistently named the best street food in all of New York—it even gets reviewed in *The New York Times*! Taquitos, huaraches, tamales, pupusas, quesadillas—just look at what everyone else is ordering and follow suit. You'll go home full and happy.

- **Beard St. Pier**, *Van Brunt and Beard Streets.*
- **Brooklyn Waterfront Artists Coalition (BWAC)**, *718-596-2507, www.bwac.org.*
- **Red Hook Waterfront Arts Festival**, *Contact Dance Theatre Etcetera, 718-643-6790, www.dancetheatreetcetera.org.*
- **Queen Mary 2**, *schedule, www.cunard.com.*
- **Hudson Waterfront Museum**, *290 Conover St. at Pier 44, 718-624-4719, www.waterfrontmuseum.org.*
- **Steve's Authentic Key Lime Pies**, *Pier 41 Van Dyke St. bet. Cononer and Ferris Sts., www.stevesauthentic.com.*

- **Baked**, *359 Van Brunt St., bet. Wolcott and Dykeman Sts., 718-222-0345, www.bakednyc.com.*
- **Red Hook ballfields**, *most food vendors near intersection of Bay and Clinton Sts.*
- **Getting there:** *F or G to Smith and 9th St., then B77 bus to corner of Van Dyke and Van Brunt. A, C, or F to Jay St./Borough Hall, then B61 to Van Brunt (last stop).*

Midtown Lite
Radio City Music Hall tour...Channel Gardens...Top of the Rock...Ziegfeld Theatre...NBA Store...waterfalls...Ellen's Stardust Diner.

Save this trip for a day when you're prepared to spend a bit of money to get a bit of pampering. The first stop: **Radio City Music Hall** for a tour (which you can take any time except Christmas or Easter). It may seem corny, but people report near-spiritual feelings at the sight of that gorgeous place up close and empty. In the course of forty-five minutes, you will study Radio City's interior architecture, the Mighty Wurlitzer, the proscenium arch, the backstage areas, and the complex workings of the stage; kids will look at those big gears and murmur, "Awesome!" Some call it a wonder of the world; you might call it $17 per adult and $10 per child well spent.

Afterwards, mosey over to Rockefeller Center's **Channel Gardens**, so-called because they separate La Maison Francaise and the British Empire Building (but you knew that). Check out the skaters if it's winter and pay your respects to the Prometheus Sculpture. If you feel like shopping, take the glass-enclosed elevator down from the rink to the lower level. Children will love the ant-colony feel of the bustling concourse, and you will have many choices for food and souvenirs (excellent Statues of Liberty made of some green polymer-like substance on a white marble-like base).

The coolest thrill around here, in our opinion, is the reopened **Top of the Rock** observation deck on the 67th, 69th and 70th floors of 30 Rockefeller Plaza. The 70th-floor level is breathtakingly unenclosed, and when you look south, the Empire State Building is right there, as you've never before seen it. The decks themselves are Deco, and have a strangely tranquil feel—absolutely worth the price of admission!

The next luxurious stop is a movie at the **Ziegfeld Theatre.** This is excessive and thrilling in its gigantic way, with all the Dolby sound and tall escalators and blockbuster movies and exorbitant Raisinets. It's pricier than your local multiplex, but here, your shoes do not meld with the gum on the floor and you don't hear other movies playing on either side of you.

The young hoops fan will relish a look into the **NBA Store**, with basketball arcade games and balls you can chuck through actual hoops while deciding which of the basketball-related mugs, key rings, totes, T-shirts, etc., to buy.

Now take in an odd **waterfall** (it's free!). Head down Sixth to 49th Street and turn west along the side of the McGraw-Hill building. Just behind it, you'll see a little park. Investigate and you will find yourself walking through a water tunnel to 48th Street, with (glass-enclosed) water cascading around your head and down beside you. The experience is strangely calming.

Finally, dispel whatever feelings of repose you may have just engendered with a visit to **Ellen's Stardust Diner** at 51st Street and Broadway. How to explain this place? It's a fantasy of a '50s diner—all chrome and booths, with a jukebox, TV screens, and waiters in loudly patterned vests. The menu is comfort food of many lands—everything from fajitas to french fries. Your children will happily chow down on the shakes and malteds, sliders, sandwiches, or chicken potpie. Then there's the little train that goes steadily chugging high up around the perimeter, and, if you go there after 7 p.m. any night from Wednesday through Saturday, you'll be treated to the sights and sounds of singing waitpersons. As New Yorkers, we're used to actor-waiters, but not that many of them can belt out a Sondheim tune. Oldies on the TV, maybe a lime rickey—and that train. How could you deny your kids this seminal experience?

- **Radio City Music Hall**, *1260 Ave. of the Americas at 50th St., 212-632-4041, www.radiocity.com.*

- **Rockefeller Center**, *47th-51st Sts., bet. 5th and 6th Aves., 212-632-3975, www.rockefellercenter.com.*
- **The Channel Gardens**, *Fifth Ave. bet. 49th and 50th Sts.*
- **Top of the Rock**, *30 Rockefeller Plaza, entrance on 50th St., bet. 5th and 6th Aves. (Hours: 8:00 a.m. to midnight, last elevator goes up at 11:00 p.m.), www.topoftherock-nyc.com.*
- **Ziegfeld Theatre**, *141 W. 54th St., bet. 6th and 7th Aves., 212-777-FILM ext. 602.*
- **NBA Store**, *666 Fifth Ave., bet. 52nd and 53rd Sts., 212-515-6221, www.nba.com/nycstore.*
- **McGraw-Hill Building**, *1221 Avenue of the Americas bet. 48th and 49th Sts.*
- **Ellen's Stardust Diner**, *1650 Broadway at 51st St., 212-956-5151, www.ellensstardustdiner.com.*
- **Getting there:** *B, D, F, or V to Rockefeller Center.*

Chapter Six

action without angst:

venues and activities

Sometimes you need to take the kids to a place where there are lots of things to choose from; sometimes they know what they want to do and just need a great place to do it. Accordingly, this chapter has two sections: First, our favorite multipurpose facilities; then, our top picks for specialized interests.

1. Everything in One Place

Four Words: New York City Parks

Consider what you can do in them: baseball, cricket, field hockey, football, soccer, croquet, bird-watching, basketball, golf, lawn bowling, bocce, row-boating and canoeing, model-yacht-sailing, nature walks, track and field, astronomy, paddle ball, cycling, curling, rollerblading, fishing, horseback riding, ice skating, wall climbing, rock climbing, and swimming.

Did we mention softball, haunted walks and hay rides (in season), Buddhist meditations, winter fairs, equestrian fairs, Highland games, Easter egg rolls, square dances, yoga classes, chess, checkers, children's theater and dance? Let's not forget traditional pleasures such as feeding the ducks, rolling down hills, and picnicking.

Absolutely the best way to find out what's going on is to be in touch with the Urban Park Rangers. They're courteous and very knowledgeable—and they send out free mailing lists. Like the parks themselves, they are a resource no parent should ever underestimate.

By the way, did we leave out free Shakespeare? Call 311 or visit www.nycgovparks.org.

Chelsea Piers

Despite its smooth publicity, which makes some cool parents wary, this place is well-run and can be a nice experience for you and your kids. Sky Rink's two indoor skating rinks are spacious, clean, and light-filled (and on a boiling August day, perfect!), with their big windows looking out over the Hudson. Of course, you can sign the children up for all kinds of classes and leagues, but if you just want to give them something pleasantly active to do for an afternoon, with no strings attached, you have several options: open basketball games (pay by the hour), baseball, soccer, batting cages, gymnastics, rock climbing, bowling, roller-skating or blading (on either of two outdoor roller rinks), and hitting balls off a tee on the driving range (in the golf club, which has kid-size clubs). The Toddler Adventure Center is a great indoor play area for the littlest ones.

- **Chelsea Piers**, *23rd St. and the Hudson River. For information, call 212-336-6666, or www.chelseapiers.com.*
- **Getting there:** *C or E train to 23rd St., then walk west to the river or take the M23 bus west.*

Aviator Sports and Recreation

Attention, fans of deepest Brooklyn and Queens! There's a huge and spiffy new facility at Floyd Bennett Field. Floyd Bennett was New York City's first airport, used by Amelia Earhart and famed as "Wrong Way" Corrigan's point of departure. It then became an army field and has over the years been used as a training ground for EMS and police drivers as well as for occasional events (the most important of which, for our purposes, is Native American Indian Powwows (p. 70).

Now, in and around four of the original (carefully restored) hangars, this sports complex houses two ice rinks, a thirty-five-foot climbing wall, basketball courts, a gymnastics and dance center, a fitness center and two outdoor turf fields for football, soccer, and lacrosse. You can drop in, join a league, watch a game (lots of teams use the facility), hold a birthday party, or go to summer camps here. You can play dodgeball and whiffleball too!

Whatever brings you out here, be sure to visit the food court, which features Brooklyn specialties of the best kind. We're talking pizza made by the legendary Patsy Grimaldi of Grimaldi's Pizzeria in DUMBO (see p. 90) and offered at $2.50 a slice. (This will thrill and astonish diehard fans of the restaurant, where slices are definitely not on the menu.) Also Jacques Torres chocolate and Junior's cheesecake. What could be bad?

Before you leave, ponder this: Floyd Bennett Field is part

of the sprawling Gateway National Recreation Area, and is the only place in New York City where your family can go outdoor camping accompanied by a ranger, all gear supplied.

- **Aviator Sports and Recreation**, *Floyd Bennett Field, Hangar 5, Brooklyn, 718-758-9800, www.aviatorsports.com.*
  For outdoor camping at Floyd Bennett Field, contact Urban Outback at 718-338-4306.
- **Getting there:** *2 or 5 train to the Flatbush Avenue/Brooklyn College station (last stop), Q35 bus one block from the train station (at Flatbush Ave. between Nostrand Avenue and Avenue H). Request bus driver to stop across from Aviator Sports and Recreation at Floyd Bennett Field. Aviator Sports complex is in the hangars to the left of the Ryan Visitor Center.*

2. Special Interests

Around and Around: Carousels

This is one of the few rides children and their parents can sincerely enjoy together. Carousels are safe and easy, they make everyone smile, and they go surprisingly fast, so you should never pass up a chance to climb onto one. Here's where to find them in New York:

Central Park: Located at 65th Street, mid-park. This one can be so full of courting couples and sensitive singles, you'd think children weren't allowed on, but they are. (www.central-park.com.)

Bryant Park's is the most centrally located, and, although it's only been in place since 2002, looks gloriously turn-of-the-century. (www.bryantpark.org.)

Riverbank's Totally Kid Carousel is the city's most idiosyncratic, the mounts based on drawings done by local children. At 145th Street at the Hudson River. (212-694-3600.)

Prospect Park. Beautifully restored and just south of the Prospect Park Wildlife Center (formerly known as the Zoo) (www.prospectpark.org.)

In Queens, there are two, one in **Flushing Meadows** at 111th Street and Fourth Avenue (718-592-6539), and another in **Forest Park** at Woodhaven Boulevard and Park Lane (718-805-5572). (www.nycgovparks.org.)

Coming attractions: Coney Island's B&B Carousel. This beauty (complete with a brass ring) dates back to the 1920s and most recently lived in a dingy shed under the elevated train tracks at Coney. It's currently being refurbished by the city and in time it will take pride of place in the revamped amusement park. **Jane's Carousel**, now on display in DUMBO (see p. 91) is scheduled to be part of the Brooklyn Bridge Park. For information visit www.brooklynbridgepark.org.

Miniature Golf

Sometimes you just feel the need to do this even though you're not on vacation, and the city does present a few opportunities:

Randall's Island in the East River should be at the top of your list since it has two 18-hole courses. Go to www.golfandsportsinfo.com/randallsisland/minigolf/html for information. For directions, visit nycgovparks.org.

Flushing Meadows-Corona Park in Queens has an 18-hole course with some enjoyably tricky aspects. It's also the only mini-golf course in New York City with night lights. You'll find it next to the U.S. Tennis Center, 718-271-8182. To get there, take the 7 train to Willets Point/Shea Stadium.

Turtle Cove Golf and Baseball Complex is a nice but not particularly manicured little place at the entrance to City Island (it also has batting cages and a driving range). Afterwards, you can go to one of the seafood restaurants on City Island Avenue for clams! Turtle Cove Golf and Baseball Complex, 1 City Island Rd., the Bronx, 718-885-2646.

Coming attraction: A new and improved mini-golf park is in development on the Hudson River at Pier 25 (off North Moore Street). Check www.hudsonriverpark.org for updates.

Rollerblading and Skateboarding

All over the city teenagers find places to hone these skills, whether or not they're allowed to, but there are an increasing number of places where they can do so without annoying anyone. Here are some:

Along the Hudson: This is probably the most inviting place to blade or board in the whole city and there are places to do both—all the way from the Battery up to Riverside Park. However, the waterfront is always crowded; bladers have to share the available space with cyclists and pedestrians and things can get intense. For savvy insider advice, check out The New York City Inline Skating Guide for Manhattan South (www.skatecity.com/nyc/where/manhattans.html) and then pick a beautiful day for your excursion.

Under the Unisphere: This is not an official venue but so adored that it might as well be. It's at the site of the World's Fair in Flushing Meadows Corona Park, Queens (see p. 34). You'll see some extremely fancy trick skating here.

Courtesy of The New York City Parks Department: It operates skateboard/rollerblade/bike parks in all five boroughs. They're well-designed, safe and clean. Our favorite is **Millennium Skate Park** in Owl's Head Park, Brooklyn. Why? Because it's high up above the Belt Parkway and New York Harbor is spread out below. Just over the Belt, reachable via several footbridges, is Shore Road Park, the narrow ribbon of green that runs between the parkway and the water. Fishermen, bladers, and cyclists are out in force in all weather. And not too far away, on a bench closer to the Verrazano-Narrows Bridge, John Travolta won Karen Lynn Gorney's heart, not to mention our own, in *Saturday Night Fever*. Don't even bother trying to explain it to Junior; you'll only embarrass yourself. For the skate park, enter Owl's Head Park at Colonial Road and Wakeman Place.

For more information on and directions to all the skateboard/rollerblade/bike parks in the city go to www.nycgov-parks.org and click on "Things to Do."

Outdoor Ice-skating

One of the joys of living in New York is the occasional moment when you do something that makes you feel you're in a movie (as opposed to stepping around one that's being filmed, annoyingly, on your way to the subway). Outdoor ice-skating is one of those experiences. There's nothing like the thrill of, say, the Rockefeller Center rink in the snow. (Remember that lovely last scene in *Christmas Eve on Sesame Street*?) These are the rinks in the city's parks:

- **Manhattan**
  Central Park's Lasker Rink, 107th St., 917-492-3856, www.nycgov.parks.org.
  Wollman Rink, 63rd St., 212-439-6900, www.wollman-skatingrink.com.
  Bryant Park, bet. 40th and 42nd Sts. and 5th and 6th Aves., 866-221-5157, www.thepondatbryantpark.com.
  Rockefeller Center, call 212-332-7654 or visit www.rap-atina.com/iceRink.

- **Brooklyn**
  Prospect Park's Kate Wollman Rink on East Dr. near Parkside and Ocean Ave. This is due for a complete renovation and overhaul—and a second rink—from Spring 2008–2010. 718-287-6431, www.prospectpark.org.
  Abe Stark Rink on the Coney Island boardwalk at W. 19th St. 718-946-6536.

- **Queens**
  World's Fair Rink, in Flushing Meadows Corona Park. A truly fabulous location. 718-271-1996.

- **Staten Island**
  War Memorial Rink, Clove Lakes Park, Victory Blvd. and Clove Rd., 718-720-1010. For directions, go to www.nyc-govparks.org.

*P.S. As part of its holiday festivities, the **South Street Seaport** usually installs a rink right next to the ships. Like some New York apartments, it makes up in location what it lacks in size. www.southstreetseaport.com.*

3. For the Birds

Migrations

Because of its strategic location on migratory flight paths, New York City is visited seasonally by everything from herons to hawks to weird little warblers, the mere mention of which gets enthusiasts' phone wires humming. At almost any time of year, Urban Park Rangers conduct bird-watching expeditions in parks all over the city. Call 311 to find out more. The real thrill comes in the early spring or fall when masses and masses of birds are on the move. When this happens, take your young naturalists to the **Ramble in Central Park**, thirty-seven acres of woods and streams that the birds consider a very desirable location (after all, it's Manhattan), and the **Jamaica Bay Wildlife Refuge**, which is part of the **Gateway National Recreation Area**.

Jamaica Bay Wildlife Refuge, 718-318-4340, www.nps.gov. Tours are free, and last up to two hours; there are picnic tables (but no food) and toilets in the Visitors' Center.

Getting there: Even if you don't have a car, you can reach this enormous stretch of marsh, dune, and water by subway and foot. Here's how: Put on walking shoes, pack binoculars (and snacks, and a picnic), and take the A train to Far Rockaway. Your stop is Broad Channel. From the subway, walk one block west to Cross Bay Boulevard and then north three-quarters of a mile to the entrance to the Refuge. (This distance rules out the tinies.)

Pale Male

The celebrity red-tailed hawk has been the focus of paparazzi since 1993, when he first arrived, found a mate, and began raising chicks on Fifth Avenue. Now, at least four mates, twenty-six fledglings, and a couple of nests later—and after a hugely entertaining battle *royale* with his neighbors—he lives with the lovely Lola in specially designed quarters at 927 Fifth and 74th Street. The two start to mate sometime in February and seem to do it all over the neighborhood. From then until sometime in May, you can watch their comings and goings at the nest and marvel as the eggs hatch and the fledglings learn to fly. You'll also see them nearby in the park, often at the Model Sailboat Pond or the Ramble. Needless to say, Pale Male has his own website: www.palemale.com. PBS made a wonderful *Nature* movie about the bird and his fans, called *Pale Male*. Why not rent it from Netflix?

The Brooklyn Parrots
There are lots of these sweet little green birds nesting on the light towers at the Brooklyn College playing fields and at various Flatbush street corners. The most scenic and elaborate nests are tucked into the latticed stonework of Green-Wood Cemetery's Gothic Revival entrance gate. People have put forward many theories as to how they got here but the consensus is that it was some kind of a breakout. Good for them! They're Brooklynites now.

- **Green-Wood Cemetery**, 500 25th St., Brooklyn, 718-768-7300, www.green-wood.com.
- **Getting there:** R to 25th St. and walk to 25th St. and Fifth Ave.

downtime:
great new york movies
that you can watch
happily with your kids,
at least for the first
eight or ten times

Ghostbusters (1984)—Maybe too scary for the tinies, but a script loaded with zingers and exuberant, laugh-out-loud set pieces, anchored by the teamwork of Bill Murray, Dan Ackroyd, Harold Ramis, and Rick Moranis. **Ghostbusters 2** (1989) isn't as funny or as charming, but it's still got the cast, the raucous New York atmosphere, and a walking Statue of Liberty.

Guys and Dolls (1955)—Frank Sinatra before sainthood, Marlon Brando before statehood, Times Square before porn or gentrification. Purists may carp that Marlon is playing Frank's role and can't sing, but it still has the greatest, most joyous score of them all, a wonderful supporting cast (viva Vivian Blaine and Stubby Kaye!), great sets and costumes, and foist-class Noo Yawk accents.

King Kong (1933)—The world's most soulful ape maintains his dignity even when hanging off the Empire State Building, and Fay Wray can really scream. The film has a special relevance for today, when kids' bathsoap comes in endangered species shapes. Note: Insist on the original! The 1976 and 2005 versions just don't compare.

Miracle on 34th Street (1947)—Santa Claus comes to town and finds it full of doubters, cynics, and skeptics. This Christmas fable tempers its sentimentality with a nice dose of city wit, but cool parents and kids alike will melt as Edmund Gwenn makes everyone's Christmas dreams come true. Younger children will fade during some of the romantic longueurs. Catch the shots of Macy's Thanksgiving Day Parade before television, commercialism, and balloon technology transformed it; here, it might as well be a small-town parade. Even though this is on TV endlessly during the holidays, rent it; it's much, much better without commercials. And make sure it's the 1947 original, not the appalling 1994 remake with Richard Attenborough.

On the Town (1949)—Sure, the patter's a little sluggish and the musical numbers overlong, but the opening ("New York, New York") is heaven and the Manhattan location shots are fascinating (catch Columbus Circle without the Time Warner Center). As for Frank (Sinatra), Gene (Kelly), Ann (Miller), Betty (Garrett), and Jules (Munshin)—they are sheer bliss to watch.

Searching for Bobby Fischer (1993)—Based on a true story, this movie about an American chess prodigy who gets his start among the patzers of Washington Square makes the ancient game seem as cool as hoops.

Spider-Man (2002) and ***Spider-Man 2*** (2004)—Earnest, geeky, and insecure, Spidey fights crime while going to college, holding down a part-time job and looking after Aunt May. Not bad for a kid from Queens. These films combine believable characters, juicy villains, exciting storylines and extravagant effects along with plenty of NYC scenery and attitude. Remember the spectacular scene in the first movie with Spidey, the Goblin, and a swaying Roosevelt Island tram full of terrified people? *Spider-Man 2* is a true rarity, a sequel that's better than its predecessor. The third installment falls short, but number four is on its way.

Superman: The Movie (1978) and ***Superman II*** (1980)— Christopher Reeves' graceful and witty bow as the Man of Steel. Farewell baggy tights and dopey flying effects, hello Margot Kidder and a raft of terrific character actors, including Marlon Brando, Valerie Perrine, and Gene Hackman, whose hideout is located in the bowels of Grand Central Station. *Superman II;* much of which was shot at the same time as the first; is just as good, which is to say better than any of the successors.

Tootsie (1982)—Dustin Hoffman's finest hour as a starving actor who becomes a soap opera diva. As sweet as it is hilarious, this gender-bender also features fine contributions from Bill Murray, Terri Garr, Jessica Lange, Dabney Coleman, and Charles Durning.

A Tree Grows in Brooklyn (1945)—Elia Kazan's first film demonstrates his always extraordinary work with actors. A four-hankie weeper set in Williamsburg, Brooklyn, around the turn of the (last) century, this story of a loving family and its tribulations is best for older children, who will love the views of children at play in a bygone New York (especially the Christmas tree scene). The brilliant child actress Peggy Ann Garner will steal your heart.

West Side Story (1961)—If only juvenile delinquency were really this way. This urban *Romeo and Juliet* will squeeze tears from anyone old enough to follow the plot. The exteriors were shot where Lincoln Center stands today.

The World of Henry Orient (1964)—About a Brooklyn con artist turned foreign-born concert pianist and the two pre-adolescent girls who worship him. Peter Sellers is inspired as Henry. Tippy Walker is delightful as the more troubled of the two girls, and Angela Lansbury is an excellent villainess. Central Park in winter has never looked lovelier.

Note: As of this writing, all of these films are available on dvd. Some of them (i.e., *Searching for Bobby Fischer*, *West Side Story*) may be over the heads of smaller children. Then again, maybe not. As cool parents, you know what is or isn't appropriate fare for your family.

eight suggestions for connoisseurs of cool

As a cool parent, it's exciting to discover some great new place, some new thing to do—even though it's embarrassing when you discover that it's been there all along without you even noticing. In a city as protean as New York, it happens. Here are eight old and new discoveries:

1. Dawn Chorus—Chinese Fighting Thrushes at the Hua Mei Bird Garden

Every day from around 7 a.m. until noon, a group of Chinese men, most elderly, bring their cherished birds to this little fenced-off section of Sara Delano Roosevelt Park. There are all kinds of exotic and colorful species here; the smaller ones have the look of finches or canaries. The stars are the fighting thrushes, big and brown with bluish-white rings around their eyes, graceful white "eyebrows," and an incredibly loud and vigorous song, which you can hear all the way to Delancey Street. They hop about inside beautifully carved bamboo cages, which their owners hang from posts or nylon line or place carefully on the ground among the trees and shrubs. The more the thrushes hear the neighboring birds, the more they experiment with their own songs; that's what the owners want, since they enter their birds in competitions.

The result is a chorus of heavenly sounds in a green oasis just off the Manhattan Bridge. Our advice: go on a lovely weekend morning, when there could be fifty or more birds vocalizing. Be respectful, since the men (all of whom seem to be smoking like chimneys) are very serious about their passion, and keep voices low, because loud noises—other than their own—make the birds uncomfortable. Why not treat yourselves to dim sum in Chinatown before heading home?

- **The Hua Mei Bird Garden**, *Sara Delano Roosevelt Park, south of Delancey St., bet. Forsyth and Chrystie Sts., Manhattan.*
- **Getting there:** *F to Second Ave., cross Houston St., and continue walking down Chrystie St. for three blocks and then left onto Delancey St.; J, M, or Z to Bowery and walk east on Delancey for a block and a half.*

2. NYPD True—New York City Police Museum

The New York City Police Museum contains the world's largest collection of police apparatus and memorabilia, much of it absolutely irresistible to kids: handcuffs, helmets, police vehicles, and lots of firearms, from flintlock pistols to Al Capone's terrifying tommy gun. Stand in a line-up and learn how to spot a counterfeit bill. Everyone will be impressed by the lurid black-and-white photos of old-time mobsters (some post-rubout!), the sawed-off shotgun in the violin case, and the grim arsenal of weapons confiscated from juveniles: zip guns, machetes, a screw-studded baseball bat. There is also an exhibit that chronicles the NYPD's valor on 9/11, as well as displays of uniforms, badges, and arm patches.

- **New York City Police Museum**, *100 Old Slip (between Water and South Sts.), 212-480-3100, www.nycpolicemuseum.org.*
- **Getting there:** *1 or 9 to South Ferry; 2 or 3 to Wall St.; 4 or 5 to Bowling Green; J, M, or Z to Broad St.; R or W to Whitehall, South Ferry.*

3. Slots of Fun—The Buzz-a-Rama Experience

Brooklyn kids-in-the-know have made the trek to this dingy, thrilling establishment in Kensington since the dawn of the '60s. Slot-car racing involves seven-inch racing cars—steered by your children—hurtling down a 155-foot swooping, curving, silver track with grooved lanes (or slots) at speeds of up to 100 miles an hour. In 1966, there were forty such places in New York. Buzz-a-Rama is the last, and its quietly fanatical owner, Frank "Buzz" Perri, is not planning to close it any time soon. For birthday parties and special occasions, Perri can be persuaded to plug in his spectacular collection of pinball machines. Call before going; Buzz-a-Rama has no regular hours, but arrangements can usually be made.

- **Buzz-a-Rama 500**, *69 Church Ave. at Dahill Rd., Brooklyn, 718-853-1800.*
- **Getting there:** *F to Church Ave.*

4. Divine Pastime—Cathedral Church of St. John the Divine

Begun in 1892, the Cathedral Church of St. John the Divine is still unfinished; when it is, it'll be the biggest cathedral in the world, combining Gothic majesty with New York references in a way that tickles kids. After gaping up at the towering nave and the Rose Window, go outside and look at the stone carvings on the building's west front. Next to Biblical figures, you'll find images of the city carved by city kids who've been trained by English craftsmen to become contemporary stonemasons. There are guided tours Tuesdays through Saturdays at 11 a.m., and on Sundays at 1 p.m. On Saturdays, the cathedral hosts medieval arts workshops for young children (and their parents). Sculpt a clay gargoyle, chisel away at a block of stone, make your own illuminated letter using tracing paper and real gold leaf, do a brass rubbing, weave at two looms (and take home a small cardboard loom of your own) and, finally, create a stained-glass collage with tissue paper. This is a great workshop in an incredibly atmospheric location—and if it's a hit, you can book it for a birthday.

- **The Cathedral Church of St. John the Divine**, *1047 Amsterdam Ave., bet. Cathedral Parkway and W. 113th St., 212-932-7347, www.stjohndivine.org.*
- **Getting there:** *1 to 110th St.; B or C to Cathedral Parkway.*

5. Spin (and Leap and Lunge and Jump) City—S.L.A.M.

Elizabeth Streb's choreography is as much about acrobatics and gymnastics as dance. She calls her style of movement "pop action," and it's vigorous, athletic, and gravity-defying. It's earned her a MacArthur "Genius" Grant as well as the bated breath of audiences world-wide. Her studio, in a former mustard factory in Williamsburg, Brooklyn (where else?), is called S.L.A.M. (Streb Lab for Action Mechanics). A raw space with a twenty-seven-foot-high ceiling, it's cluttered with mats, scaffolding, trapezes, pulleys, and mysterious pieces of equipment designed for the express purpose of letting people move in ways that gravity would not ordinarily permit. S.L.A.M. is a thrilling place to visit—and you can.

The Streb studio is open to the public any time that staff is there, which means that you can watch the muscular dancers in rehearsal, practicing their exhilarating moves at close range. How cool is that? During breaks, they loll around eating lunch like normal people instead of the athletic daredevils they are. There are Pop Action classes throughout the week for age groups ranging from eighteen months (!) to adult, and trapeze classes under the auspices of the España-Streb Trapeze Academy. The teachers are very gentle with the kids and safety is a prime concern.

- **Streb for Action Mechanics (S.L.A.M.)** *and* **España/Streb Trapeze Academy**, *51 N. 1st St., Brooklyn, 718-384-6491. Call or check the Streb Web sites, www.strebusa.org and www.espanastrebtrapeze.org, for schedule.*
- **Getting there:** *L to Bedford, exit Bedford/N. 7th St. Walk south on Bedford, right on N. 1st St. S.L.A.M. is located between Wythe and Kent Sts.*

6. Abracadabra, etc.—Tannen's Magic

It's the largest magic shop in the world (8,000-plus tricks in stock), and professionals are always in evidence, shopping and kibitzing. Still, beginners of all ages are welcome at Tannen's Magic. The salespeople are all magicians and will happily demonstrate tricks—but only once, because customers who figure out tricks tend not to buy them. A beginner's magic set costs $70, but you can spend much less. The Spooky the Ghost Handkerchief, for instance, sells for $10. Private lessons and classes are available, and there's a week-long magic camp in August.

- **Tannen's Magic, Inc.**, *45 W. 34th St., Suite 608, 212-929-4500, www.tannens.com.*
- **Getting there:** *B, D, F, Q, R, or V to 34th St., Herald Square.*

7. Tom Otterness's Sculptures at the 14th St./Eighth Ave. subway station

You probably haven't considered spending a couple of hours in a subway station with your children, but that's exactly what we're recommending. One of the hands-down coolest and most appealing art exhibits in the entire city can be found in the large, but otherwise unprepossessing, subway station at Eighth Avenue and 14th Street, which actually extends all the way to 16th. Tom Otterness, the man responsible for the whimsical bronze figures of people and animals at Nelson A. Rockefeller Park downtown (see p. 65), created around 135 funky little figures specifically for this station. You'll see them plodding down the stairs, climbing up columns, chasing each other down the platforms, and trying to bend the iron entrance railings. The most famous of these denizens is an alligator emerging from underground to gnaw on the pants of an alarmed gent (and who can blame him?), but there's every kind of droll situation and a hefty dose of social commentary (class, money) for those who are minded to notice. See how many you can count.

After surfacing at 14th Street, go four blocks south and one block west to the fabled **Myers of Keswick**, a tight little island of Britannia in the heart of Greenwich Village. Robert Myers, the proprietor, is a butcher, and his sausages and meat pies are truly fabulous. More important for your kids is his impressive stock of English candy: Smarties, Rowntree's Fruit Gums, and Crunchie bars. Afficionados of salty snacks will thrill to the wide selection of Walker's Crisps (potato chips to us) and the Twiglets (sort of like pretzels, but much, much better). Everyone can nosh happily on the way home.

P.S. You could go exploring and find other Otternesses in locations as varied as Roosevelt Island and Times Square. For more information, go to the artist's website (www.tomostudio.com).

P.P.S. And remember, there is other art all over the subway system, most of it accessible and eye-catching.

- **Tom Otterness Subway Sculptures**: *14th St./8th Ave. stop.*
- **Myers of Keswick**, *634 Hudson St., bet. Horatio and Jane Sts., 212-691-4194, www.myersofkeswick.com.*
- **Getting there:** *A, C, E, or L to 14th St.*

8. Up, Up, and Away: The Superhero Supply Store

At first glance, it could be an old hardware store down on its luck. There are a few items and posters announcing specials in the window. The display looks half-hearted or unfinished and the sign across the top of the window is so crowded with dense writing that an extra panel extends down to ground level. All in all, it doesn't look very promising. Then you notice what the products are: cans of invisibility and chaos, utility belts, capes, and grappling hooks (a Sidekick Special, available in red only). Free mask and cowl assessments are offered. The overhead sign promises, "We can solve your nemesis problem," while a smaller sign discreetly requests that customers refrain from using their X-ray vision inside the store. What is this?!

It's Brooklyn Superhero Supply, an ingenious shop that caters to the child's inner superhuman-crusader-against-evil within. The store itself is something of a do-gooder. It is actually a front for 826NYC, a nonprofit organization founded by novelist Dave Eggers and devoted to developing writing skills and fostering creativity (everything from novel-writing to film-making) among children ages 6–18. It pursues these goals through free drop-in tutoring during the week and on Sundays, when tutors, most of them volunteers, are on hand to help kids with their homework or their writing skills in general. They work behind a "secret" panel in the store which swings open to reveal a spacious room with big tables, plenty of chairs, and all the usual detritus of kids doing creative work: colored paper, props, puppets, etc.

Even casual visitors will be charmed by this place. Remember, there are no action figures or comic books here, only what you'd need if you actually were a superhero. That means capes (you can stand on a little pedestal as a fan machine makes your cape billow out behind you), suction pads, and more. You can also buy a very nice T-shirt; the proceeds go to support the organization. Customers are required to take an oath to combat evil before making their purchases, but no one seems to object.

There are all sorts of restaurants in the area (not to mention Zuzu's Petals, a great plant and flower shop, which is next door). Among the kid-friendliest: **The Chip Shop**, one block to your right and across the street, has great fish and chips and other sturdy English specialties such as shepherd's pie, mushy peas, and a wide array of deep-fried candy bars (not a typo). It also has a children's menu. Turning left out of **Superhero Supply**, you are but one block from **Willie's Dawgs**, a bright and airy little place decorated with a hot dog mural, lots of dog figurines, and photographs, some of which depict animals you can adopt. The hot dogs include several types of all-beef weiners (Mutt and Pedigree), the "Downward-Facing Dog" (tofu and said to be excellent of its kind) and even a carrot marinated in hot dog spices before being grilled and slapped onto your choice of home-made buns (challah, multi-grain, rye). There are plenty of toppings, different mustards, good fries, Yonah Shimmel knishes, and a garden out back where you can nosh al fresco on a New York classic done right.

Head one block over to **J.J. Byrne Park** and the **Old Stone House**, originally built in 1699 and reconstructed, almost but not quite where it originally stood. It was the center of fierce fighting during the Battle of Brooklyn, the first large-scale engagement of the Revolutionary War and in 1883, it served as the clubhouse for the original Brooklyn (Trolley) Dodgers. Now it's been sweetly reconfigured as a museum and storytelling venue for children. Afterward, watch some serious handball or let the kids frolic in the playground. In October, there's a Harvest Festival with animals to pet, pony rides, and face painting, just like in colonial times (not).

- **Brooklyn Superhero Supply**, *372 Fifth Ave., Brooklyn,* *718-499-9884,*
  www.superherosupplies.com and www.826nyc.org.
- **Old Stone House Historic Center**, *Fifth Ave., bet 3rd*

and 4th Sts, J.J. Byrne Park, Brooklyn, 718-768-3195, www.theoldstonehouse.org.

- **The Park Slope Chip Shop**, 383 Fifth Ave. at 6th St., Brooklyn, 718-832-7701 (718-CHIPSHOP), www.chip-shopnyc.com.
- **Willie's Dawgs**, 351 Fifth Ave., Brooklyn, 718-832-2941.
- **Getting there:** R to Union St. and 4th Ave.; F, M, or R to 4th Ave. and 9th St.

nine places to visit and things to do for which no parent should ever be too cool

1. *Don't be too cool to join the tourists at the* **Radio City Christmas Spectacular**.
Why? Because after seventy-five years or so, it's still there. Despite its maudlin religiosity, the overpriced mega-Cokes, and the incessant drone of outlanders, this show really is the last of its kind—a gaudy spectacle of wooden soldiers, live animals, religious tableaux, and the resonant blast of the mighty Wurlitzer. If you should be fortunate enough to witness a live camel obeying the call of nature during the incredibly discreet manger scene, your children will be grateful to you forever. For you, there are the Rockettes, still alive and kicking. Afterwards, zip around the corner and take in the skyscraping Rockefeller Center Christmas tree, another astounding New York site left too long to the tourists.

- **Radio City Christmas Spectacular**, *1260 6th Ave., bet. 50th and 51st Sts., 212-307-7171. You can buy tickets online at www.christmas.radiocity.com.*
- **Getting there:** *B, D, F, or V to Rockefeller Center at 50th St.*

2. *Don't be too cool to take a round-trip ride on the* **Staten Island Ferry**.
Sure, it's a cliché, and it was more fun when you could drive on, and it used to cost a nickel. Still, the Staten Island Ferry offers one of the only world-class bargains to which New York can still lay claim. Every half hour or so, a ferry pulls away from its docking bay; half an hour or so later, it reaches its destination. Along the way, you've smelled the sea and felt its spray, cruised right by the Statue of Liberty, and experienced no seasickness. There are three new boats, but most look old, battered, and wonderful, with vintage linoleum in patterns that haven't been made for thirty years and wooden benches worn dark and smooth. The food is nothing special, but hot dogs taste absolutely wonderful at sea, with breezes blowing and engines churning loudly in the background. In fact, munching as you gaze at the Manhattan skyline or Lady Liberty, you'll swear they're the best hot dogs you've ever had in your life.

- **Staten Island Ferry**, *Whitehall Terminal, 4 South St., next to Battery Park. Call 311 for schedules or go to www.siferry.com.*
- **Getting there:** *N, R, or W to Whitehall St.; 4 or 5 to Bowling Green; 1 or 9 to South Ferry; J, M, or Z to Broad St.*

3. *Don't be too cool to experience the* **Bronx Zoo** *(which is actually the International Wildlife Conservation Park).*
Don't make the mistake of bringing the kids here when they're too young to appreciate it. All too often Dad ends up with someone on his shoulders who doesn't give a damn about the life-cycle of the slow loris. How old is old enough for the zoo? A word to the wise: Don't go until your kids are so big they'd be embarrassed to have you carry them. At that age, they can enjoy the World of Darkness with its swooping bats, glittering-eye lemurs and bush babies, and, weirdest of all, the subterranean colony of naked mole rats. They can take the Bengali Express monorail and see the wild animals they've dreamt of—elephants, tigers, rhinos. They'll love the African Plains with their lions, cheetahs, and zebras. For children weary of New York's other "Wildlife Centers," where prairie dogs and otters stand in for big game, this is the real thing. The Bronx Zoo is like no other zoo in the world. (And around the holidays, there is a truly enchanting Holiday Lights show.)

- **The International Wildlife Conservation Park**, *Fordham Rd./Bronx River Parkway, Bronx, 718-367-1010, www.bronxzoo.com.*
- **Getting there:** *2 or 5 train to East Tremont Ave/West Farms Square. There is also an express bus from Manhattan. The BxM11 makes stops along Madison Avenue, between 26th and 99th Streets, then travels directly to the Zoo's Bronx River entrance (Gate B). To return, pick up the bus just outside the same gate at the MTA BxM11 sign (just before the underpass).*

4. *Don't be too cool to visit the* **American Museum of Natural History** *and the* **Rose Center for Earth and Space**.

True, New York children visit regularly on class trips, and the fourth-floor dinosaur collection is always mobbed, but how can you not visit this place as a family?

For one thing, you probably haven't been in decades, possibly not since grade school. Besides, it is as much a part of being a New York parent as buying bagels for a teething baby. And they will love, as children always do, the tableaux of prehistoric and aboriginal peoples and the old-fashioned dioramas, with their painted backdrops and taxidermied creatures. In the Discovery Room, a "museum-within-a-museum" aimed at five to twelve-year-olds, kids can piece together a prehistoric reptile's skeleton or track an earthquake. Then again, wouldn't you all rather just wander around gazing at stuff? We particularly like to gape at the splendors in the Halls of Mineral and Gems, and we always end up paying our respects to the blue whale. These days, its home in the Hall of Ocean Life is full of new interactive exhibits and dioramas. The whale still steals the show, hanging from the ceiling, as graceful and lowering as a storm cloud. The littlest children will race around the polished floor beneath it while you stare, pondering its enormity.

If you've got the energy, move on to the **Rose Center for Earth and Space**. Be warned: It's gorgeous and very high-tech, but some of its exhibits can be a little puzzling for young minds, not to mention plenty of mature ones. You can't miss, though, with the Hayden Planetarium space shows. With their spectacular visualizations and animations based on the latest data from the furthest space, these films are narrated by august stars like Robert Redford and Harrison Ford (Han Solo himself) and they succeed in making science as exciting as science fiction. The twenty-minute shows are well worth the supplementary charge, but you must book before you get there (tickets are available on a walk-up basis, but leave those to the out-of-towners; you don't need another line to wait on).

At the door you'll get a "Passport to the Universe" with a nifty hologram. Hang on to it; it'll help you remember whether the Milky Way is part of the Virgo Supercluster or vice versa. The Big Bang Theatre, downstairs, features a lot of sound and fury and Jodie Foster explaining the origin of the universe. (Don't take tiny children to this, because the bang is *really* big.) Afterwards, you walk out and down the Cosmic Pathway, which takes you through thirteen billion years of cosmic evolution. (This is the part that's challenging for many of us.)

Kids love to touch the massive and mysterious Willamette Comet in the Hall of the Universe; the nearby crater-making machine gets a lot of play, too. Best Planetarium gift-shop gimcrack: a marble-sized globe, with continents of semi-precious stones inlaid in a lapis lazuli sea.

Hungry yet? The museum's food court is large and varied, but the lines are horrendous. We prefer heading over to **E.J.'s Luncheonette**, kid-friendly home of the crisp fry, the thick shake, and the sassy waitstaff.

- **American Museum of Natural History and Rose Center for Earth and Space**, *Central Park at W. 79th St., 212-769-5100, www.amnh.org.*
- **Space Show at the Hayden Planetarium** *tickets can be purchased online at www.amnh.org or by calling 212-769-5200.*
- **E.J.'s Luncheonette**, *447 Amsterdam Ave., bet. 81st and 82nd Sts., 212-873-3444.*
- **Getting there:** *B or C to 81st Street; 1 to 79th St. and walk two blocks east.*

5. *Don't be too cool to go to the top of the* **Empire State Building**.

Maybe you visited it as a child. It's time to go again, soon, and make it a habit. Try going at dusk or on a summer night, or on a foggy day when the tips of the surrounding buildings poke through the cottony cloud cover. It's just scary enough up there for the kids to realize how high up they are; for the regular price of admission you get as far as the 86th floor. Pay a a supplement and you'll get to the 102nd floor. Unfortunately, the wonderfully odd and decrepit Guinness World Records Exhibit Hall has closed down. Don't try to compensate for this loss by taking the Skyride, a jolting, twenty-minute "big-screen flight simulator" tour of New York. It will make your younger children queasy and give you the feeling that you've been had.

P.S. Before leaving, linger in the entrance lobby for the wonderful relief image of the building on the wall, and especially for the diorama of King Kong, camera in hand, climbing the tower. And if you're ever curious about what the changing colored lights at nighttime indicate, go to the pages of *Time Out New York,* which explains the current week's light show.

- **Empire State Building**, *350 Fifth Ave. at 34th St., www.esbnyc.com.*
- **Getting there:** *B, D, F, Q, N, or R to 34th St./Herald Sq.; 6 to 33rd St.*

6. *Don't be too cool to visit the* **Statue of Liberty***.*
Getting to the statue is more of an inconvenience than it used to be. After 9/11, it was off-limits completely, and now, with increased security adding to the long lines, it might seem worth a miss. But we think not. Just allow a lot of time and take bottled water and sunhats if it's summer (waiting for the boat can be a pitiless process). These days, if you want to enter the statue, you'll have to book using a "Time Pass" reservation system; it comes free with the ferry ticket.

Once there, you'll be able to climb as far as the pedestal but no further, alas. The Parks Service maintains that the staircase to the crown, which was always open before 9/11, is too delicate to handle the volume of visitors. A spirited cadre of people opposed to this idea is still lobbying for the crown's reopening; we shall see. Anyway, seeing this icon up close is a marvelous thing and the museum has the original torch, a fragile and gorgeous thing. Don't skip the gift shop, by the way—you may even find yourself posing for pics outside in one of those dopey green foam-rubber crowns.

- **Getting there:** *Get the Statue of Liberty Ferry from the Battery. We recommend ordering your tickets in advance by calling the ferry company at 1-866-STATUE4 or online at www.statuecruises.com. And try to go off-*

season. (Apparently Christmas Eve is the lightest day of the year.) For hours of operation call 212-363-3200 or visit www.nps.gov/stli.

Note: Your ferry ticket to the Lady includes passage to Ellis Island, which is profoundly affecting. Its impact, however, depends on understanding what went on there; so we strongly recommend that you take your children there only when they are old enough—third-graders at least—to know something of the island's history and its meaning to Americans.

7. Don't be too cool to go **bowling**.
Time was when bowling was the fastest-growing family sport in the U.S., and bowling alleys sprouted all over the city the way microbreweries do today. Those days are gone. Only three bowling alleys remain in Manhattan but all feature the gutter-closing bumpers that are essential for children and all do birthday parties.

AMF Chelsea Piers Bowl has forty lanes and the ever-thrilling Xtreme Bowling-and-lights experience.

Bowlmor Lanes in Greenwich Village is a groovy '30s artifact where chic people hang out after the kids have gone home. Day-Glo pins!

The Leisure Time Bowling and Recreation Center, in the Port Authority, also has a small arcade with air hockey and video games (including Dance Dance Revolution), plenty of fast food and drink, leagues of all sorts, and the occasional celebrity-bowling event.

Outside Manhattan, bowling venues abound. For our money, the **Gil Hodges Lanes** in far-off Mill Basin, Brooklyn, is a treat worth the trip if you're going by car. It's a spacious, state-of-the-art establishment whose gutter-blockers appear at the yank of a lever from one of the lads who operate the joint. There are sixty-four lanes, baseball memorabilia on the walls (Gil Hodges himself founded this place) and perfectly decent food service (nachos, fries, and dogs). Parking is a cinch.

- **AMF Chelsea Piers Bowl**, *W. 23rd St. and West Side Highway, 212-835-2695, www.chelseapiers.com.*
- **Getting there:** *C or E train to 23rd St., then walk west to the river or take the M23 bus west.*
- **Bowlmor Lanes**, *110 University Place, 212-255-8188, www.bowlmor.com.*
- **Getting there:** *4,5,6,N,R,Q,W or L trains to 14th Str./Union Sq., then walk one and a half blocks south down University Pl.*
- **Leisure Time Bowling and Recreation Center**, *625 Eighth Ave. (at Port Authority Bus Terminal), 212-268-6909, www.leisuretimebowl.com.*
- **Getting there:** *A, C, E, N, Q, R W, 1, 2, 3 or 7 to 42nd St. and Times Square, then follow signs to Port Authority. Leisure Time is on the second floor of the south wing.*
- **Gil Hodges Lanes**, *6161 Strickland Ave., Brooklyn, 718-763-333, www.gilhodgeslanes.com.*
- **Getting there:** *Q train to Avenue U, then B3 bus to Mill Avenue and Avenue U, then walk south on Mill Ave. for a block and a half.*

8. *Don't be too cool to go on a* **day trip to the beach**.
The city beaches are funky, let's face it. Even at Jacob Riis beach, which is the best maintained, you'll find yourself at awfully close quarters with other people's music, children, and private lives. So get up very early one day and take yourselves off to Jones Beach. It, too, can be crowded; but it's a state park, with dunes, surf, and (6.5) miles of beach. It's an easy trip from Penn Station, and all you have to do once you arrive is trot down the stairs to the bus. In ten minutes or so, you'll have sand between your toes. There are optimistic buildings from the '30s; there's everything you need in terms of food, drink, and bathrooms. Remember, early is definitely best here; so that by the time the crowds are heaviest and the sun is at its most relentless, you'll be ready for home. The number for Jones Beach State Park is 516-785-1600. For train schedules and prices, call the Long Island Railroad at 718-217-5477.

9. Don't be too cool to go to ever-funky, ever-fabulous **Coney Island** *and here's why:*

You can take the subway and get out in the spanking-new, light-filled (and solar powered!) **Stillwell Avenue Station**, just across Surf Avenue from the beach.

The **Aquarium** is right nearby and a delight: sharks, seals, otters, and penguins galore, all looking laidback and well cared-for. (In June 2007, a walrus calf was born, only the tenth born in North America. He weighed 115 pounds, a husky baby if ever there was one.) There are exhibits of river and shore life, not to mention giant rays, eels, and squid for the invaluable creep factor. Call to find out about feeding times and special events. The food available for humans is adequate, but you'll be happier if you go west a few blocks for some of Coney's traditional unhealthy treats.

The rides and other tacky amusements: Right now, everything's up for grabs on this decrepit and highly desirable piece of waterfront. Some things will never change: the rickety Cyclone roller coaster, for example, and the Wonder Wheel. The Astroland kiddie rides are hanging by a thread, and the Thunderbolt coaster and the little cottage underneath it that Woody Allen immortalized in *Annie Hall* are gone. But the elegant skeleton of the Parachute Jump remains, gaudily illuminated in the summer. And you can be sure that whatever developers finally decide to do, there will always be flashy, noisy, splendid entertainments to enjoy—including the B&B Carousel.

Speaking of gaudy entertainments, look out for **Sideshows by the Seashore**, an old-fashioned freak show that is the brainchild of Dick Zigun, informally known as the Mayor of Coney Island. He's also responsible for the raucous and ever-groovy Mermaid Parade (many outrageous costumes and topless lovelies) and the New Year's Day Polar Bear Swim at which assorted doughy souls, many of them Russian, jump into the frigid sea. Sideshows run almost continuously on summer weekends, affording your children—preferably not the squeamish or little ones—a rare chance to see a sword-swallower, fire-eater, snake-charmer, contortionist, and similar specialists at a reasonable cost. In addition, Zigun says on the Sideshows website, visitors have access to "a clean bathroom, quality souvenirs, and a friendly, knowledgeable person to answer questions about the neighborhood." Is that an excellent deal or what?

The food: Snacks are everywhere, and nowhere better than at **Nathan's**, with its excellent dogs, the world's best French fries, clams, bright yellow corn and more recently, hamburgers, fish and chips, and chicken. There's a McDonald's nearby, if you have no choice. Do not hesitate on the question of cotton candy. Going home with a sticky chin is part of the deal.

Baseball by the seaside: **KeySpan Park** is the home of the Brooklyn Cyclones, who've been around since 2001 and have become adored local heroes. Get tickets much earlier than you were planning to; home games sell out right away. And bring enough money for a cap or T-shirt; the designs are fabulous.

Finally, the beach and the light and the breeze that first made Coney a resort in the 1860s. Stroll down the boardwalk, sniffing the sea air, maybe go down to the sand to dip a toe in the water, and end up at **Brighton Beach**, which is now an affluent Russian village. See how long it takes your children to notice that nobody around them is speaking English and that the graffiti is in Cyrillic script. Gape at the old-country delicacies such as caviar and sturgeon, black bread and preserves. The prices are good if you want to stock up. You and your bounty of stuffed animal prizes and seashells can catch the subway here, too, and nap on the way home.

There, have we convinced you?

- **New York Aquarium**, *Surf Ave. at W. 8th St., 718-265-3474, wcs.org/home/zoos/nyaquarium.*
- **Sideshows by the Seashore**, *1208 Surf Ave. at W. 12th St., 718-372-5101, www.coneyislandusa.com.*
- **Nathan's Famous Restaurant**, *1310 Surf Ave. at Stillwell Ave., 718-946-2202, www.nathansfamous.com.*
- **KeySpan Park**, *1904 Surf Ave., 718-449-TIXS, www.brooklyncyclones.com.*
- **Getting there:** *D, F, N, or Q train to Stilwell Ave.*

the urge to splurge:

ten treats that are fun for kids, easy for parents

- **Getting home:** *Q from Brighton Beach.*

1. The Plays Are the Thing—New Victory Theatre

The New Victory has always been ahead of its time. Built in 1900, it was first a legit playhouse, then Broadway's first burlesque theater and later its first triple-X cinema. Now it's the Great White Way's first full-time children's theater, a reliable venue for non-patronizing, quality entertainment by professional theater companies from all over the world, including Australia's sweetly anarchic Circus Oz and Louisville's distinguished Stage One. Engagements last from two to four weeks and most are geared toward children seven and up.

- **The New Victory Theatre**, *209 W. 42nd St., bet. 7th and 8th Aves., 646-223-3020, www.newvictory.org.*
- **Getting there:** *1, 2, 3, 7, N, Q, R, S, or W to Times Square.*

2. TV Winner—Paley Center for Media

Look, nobody's perfect. Sometimes, you just want to sit placidly with your kids and stare at reruns of old TV shows. Call them "classic" if it makes you feel better. Well, at this palace of nostalgia, formerly known as the Museum of Television and Radio, they do have the classics, everything from *The Ed Sullivan Show* (wanna see the Beatles' first appearance?) to *The Lone Ranger* and *I Love Lucy*. You can call up as many as four selections on the computer and watch them on a console for up to two hours. The cost is $10 for adults, $5 for children under fourteen.

- **The Paley Center for Media**, *25 W. 52nd St., bet. 5th and 6th Aves., 212-621-6600 or 212-621-6800 for tape. Call for details and to find out about special showings for children or visit www.mtr.org.*
- **Getting there:** *E or V train to Fifth Ave. and 53rd St.; B, D, F, or V to 47–50 St./Rockefeller Center.*

3. Baubles, Bangles, Bargains—The Garment District

Here's a notion: notions! Take your budding Zac Posen or

Patricia Field shopping for small and fabulous things in the Garment District. The perfect place to start is **M&J Trimmings** on Sixth Avenue: two bright, busy floors of buttons, trim, beads, fringe, tassels, ribbons...you get the idea. Check out the appliqués (which the rest of us might call patches) of dogs and bugs, flowers and fruit. Our favorites are the sequined carrot and the mohair ducky. From 38th to 42nd Streets, between Sixth and Eighth Avenues, you'll find much more wonderful stuff, from flowers and feathers to fabrics and gemstones for making jewelry. **Lace Star** has more exquisite kinds of lace than you could imagine. On weekends, we recommend regular visits to your local flea market to rummage among the ancient purses, vests, and posters or to pick up a tiny tank or old comic for $1. Your children are New Yorkers, after all, so they must learn these things.

- **M&J Trimmings**, *1008 6th Ave. bet. 37th and 38th Sts., (there's a button store, two doors down), 212-391-9072, www.mjtrim.com.*
- **Lace Star,** *215 W. 40th St., 212-840-0555 or 212-840-0440, www.lacestar.com.*

4. Venues of the Gods—Backstage at Yankee Stadium and Madison Square Garden (and why not scream yourselves hoarse at a New York Liberty game?)

These one-hour tours are a wonderful combination of insider lore (How do they keep the outfield grass so nice? Where does the ice for the Christmas show come from?) and reverent moments (in the steps of the Babe! Of Clyde!). The Classic Tour at Yankee Stadium takes you to the field, the dugout, the press box, the clubhouse, and Monument Park, with its busts and plaques commemorating The Great Ones. On MSG's All Access tours, you visit locker rooms for the Knicks, Rangers, and Liberty, go backstage at the theater and learn all the technical tidbits involved in maintaining a multi-purpose arena. And there's always the chance you'll see athletes or performers warming up. At the time of this writing, the biggest thrill at MSG has to be watching the WNBA's Liberty. Go in mid-June through August and you'll find yourself immediately enveloped in an atmosphere that's so deliriously enthusiastic and partisan that you'll be hollering along with the kids.

- **Yankee Stadium tours**, *daily at noon. Tickets can be purchased at www.yankees.com.*
- **Getting there:** *B, D, 4 to 161 Street-Yankee Stadium.*

- **Madison Square Garden**, *tours daily at various times. Price: $17 for adults, $12 for children. For tickets call Ticketmaster or go to the MSG website, www.thegarden.com. Liberty tickets can be bought through the MSG website, www.thegarden.com or www.wnba.com.*
- **Getting there:** *1, 2, 3, A, C, E to 34th Street/Penn Station. Also B, D, F, N, Q, R to 34th Street/Avenue of the Americas (one block walk).*

5. Speedboat Thrills—The Beast and the Shark

The regular Circle Line trip around Manhattan Island is a classic family outing, but it can be awfully long and too confining for kids and their ever-watchful parents. Why not cheat a bit with a couple of flashier offerings from the Circle Line? We're talking about thirty-minute dashes in gaudy speedboats with such names as The Beast and The Shark.

Leaving from Pier 83 on the West Side, The Beast races in a cloud of spray down to the Statue of Liberty and back at forty-five mph, music blaring all the way. The Shark leaves from Pier 16 at the South Street Seaport and hurtles around in the Harbor (passing by, of course, the Statue of Liberty) at similar speeds. Best view: out the front; best drenching: at the sides and a little way back. Fun, right?

- **The Beast**: *Pier 83 at W. 42nd St., 212-563-3200, www.circleline42.com.*
- **Getting there:** *A, C, or E to 42nd St./Port Authority, then walk west.*
- **The Shark**: *Pier 16 at South Street Seaport, 866-925-4631, www.circlelinedowntown.com.*

- **Getting there:** *2, 3, 4, or 5 train to Fulton St., or A or C to Broadway-Nassau. Walk east on Fulton St. to Water St. Price: Adults around $18; children (5–12) around $12. Dates: May through October.*

6. Doable Dance Concerts—the Joyce

You're going to love taking your children to Joyce Theatre. Over the years, this wonderful venue has developed a following among families looking for kid-friendly dance performances that are not *The Nutcracker*. In spring and again in the fall, the Joyce offers three family matinees at its Chelsea and Soho theaters that are designed for children but not tutu-ridden or too too cute. The dancing is uncompromisingly professional and rigorous but the approach lighthearted and appealing. The programs are so skillfully paced and varied that even the smallest children become absorbed. Tickets are reasonably priced, the vibe is comfortable and friendly, and afterwards you can meet the dancers (and get their autographs!), which is pretty thrilling for young ballerinas. If you become a member, there are big savings and other benefits.

- **The Joyce Theatre**, *75 Eighth Ave. cor. of W. 19th St., 212-242-0800, www.joyce.org.*
- **Joyce Soho**, *155 Mercer St., bet. Houston and Prince Sts., 212-431-9233. www.joyce.org.*
- **Getting there:**
  For the Joyce: A, C, or E to 14th St.; 1 to 18th St.
  For Joyce Soho: F, V, B, or D to Broadway/Lafayette; R to Prince St.; 6 to Bleecker St.

7. Fly Through the Air with the Greatest of Ease—Trapeze School

Here's a thrill: your child (no younger than six) can learn to swing on the trapeze. Even more thrillingly, the two of you can learn to partner each other in the air. No previous experience required!

It all takes place at **Trapeze School New York**, right by the water in Hudson River Park. The school works with people at

every level of expertise and confidence and is clearly successful, since this place is a hit—so much so that you must book at
least thirty days in advance. If you're hesitating, just imagine
the views you'll get from way up there. The school moves
indoors for the winter months. Check the website for details.

- **Trapeze School New York**, *Pier 40, Hudson River Park,
  West St. at Houston St., 212-242-8769,
  www.trapezeschool.com.*
- **Getting there:** *1 or 9 to Varick St., walk west to the river.*

8. Semiprecious is the Word—Astro Gallery of Gems

This is the city's best place for rocks and minerals, ranging in
size from very small to astoundingly massive. For beginners,
there are baskets of treasures for as little as $10: quartz crystals,
hunks of amethyst, and polished tumblestones like tiger's eye,
obsidian, and fool's gold. Fossil fans will love the belemites, flat
polished stones with markings of small wormy things that died
long, long ago. Our favorites are the geodes—those mysterious, jeweled caves-inside-stones. The staff is knowledgeable,
long-suffering, and helpful.

- **Astro Gallery of Gems**, *185 Madison Ave. at 34th St.,
  212-889-9000, www.astrogallery.com.*
- **Getting there:** *B, D, F, Q, N, R, V, or W to 34th
  St./Herald Square.*

9. Over There—Tram to Roosevelt Island and Back, Followed by Serendipity 3

You've gone by it and speculated about it. What are you waiting for? The tram departs from Second Avenue and 60th Street
every fifteen minutes, and at the other end you're in a quiet little town that's so unlike the city, you feel it shouldn't have a 212
area code (but it does). The excitingly ruined hospitals and asy-
lums are, alas, all fenced off, so walk north and find an open
space for sitting or picnicking or one of the numerous play-
grounds for your youngest. Then, back on the tram, and make
straight for the campy, eccentric charm of **Serendipity 3**, to
remind yourself what New York is all about. Sit elbow-to-elbow

with movie stars and their kids, tourists, and birthday cele-
brants. Go for the dishes that have stood the test of time: the
foot-long hot dogs, frozen hot chocolate, and the divine Miss
Milton's lovely fudge pie. Go crazy and buy a T-shirt, too.

- **Roosevelt Island Tramway**, *212-832-4545,
  www.rioc.com*
- **Getting there:** *4, 5, 6 to 59th Street, then walk two
  blocks east to Second Ave.*
- **Serendipity 3**, *225 E. 60th St., bet. Second and Third
  Aves., 212-838-3531, www.serendipity3.com.*
- **Getting there:** *4, 5, 6 to 59th St., then walk a block and
  a half east on 60th Street.*

10. Glass Act—UrbanGlass

UrbanGlass is a find—a glassblowing center that welcomes
children. Located in a cavernous loft-like space in downtown
Brooklyn (think: easy to get to), it hosts tours (reservations
required) and several family-friendly open houses. It's seriously
hot here, with three glowing furnaces and sweaty artists hoist-
ing globs of molten glass in and out of them. Kids can paint on
glass (which then gets fired) or create their own sandblasted
pieces of art. Just bring a glass cup or jar along and the instruc-
tors will provide stickers for decoration. The decorated items
are put into a sandblasting oven and literally bombarded with
sand particles. When they emerge, they have a chic, opaque
finish—all except for the parts covered by the stickers. Peel off
the stickers and you'll find clear glass underneath. The result is
quite impressive. Older kids might be sufficiently excited by
this hot yet cool environment to enroll in a glassblowing class,
or at least the paperweight workshop.

UrbanGlass, *647 Fulton St. (entrance at 57 Rockwell St.),
Brooklyn, 718-625-3685, www.urbanglass.org.*
Getting there: *D, M, N, Q, or R to DeKalb Ave.*